REMEMBERING...

YEARS OF HIDING
BEHIND SILENCE

CHRISTA MEINERS-DETROY

FOREWORD BY: STEVEN R. CERF

D1253567

Cover Design by Matthew Bölken DeTroy
Cover Photo: *Birch in fog.* Photo by Julie Meiners-Bölken, ca. 1940.

Photographs:
All photographs are from Christa Meiners-DeTroy's collection
or used with permission.

Library of Congress Number: 2015957112

Remembering...Years of hiding behind silence/Christa Meiners-DeTroy
p. 182
1. History :
2. Biography & Autobiography : Historical - General
I. Title.

ISBN Soft cover: 978-1-944386-00-9
ISBN Kindle: 978-1-944386-01-6

Published by:

𝒥𝒲ℬ
Just Write Books

Topsham, ME 04086
Printed in the United States of America

DEDICATION

In Memory of Rosa Abraham
and the countless victims of War and Violence

This book is also dedicated to my
children, grandchildren and great-grandchildren
to encourage them to Speak Truth to Power

CONTENTS

Seeking relatives of **Mrs. Abraham** (do not have a first name), who lived in **Worpswede**, near the city of Bremen, Germany, until the fall of 1939.
It was known that she had relatives in New York City.

Please send information to
C. DeTroy
43 Willow Grove
Brunswick, ME 04011

The advertisement the author placed tn the publication Aufbau *that garnered a response to a request for information about Mrs. Abraham.*

ACKNOWLEDGEMENTS

I am deeply grateful to my readers, Steven R. Cerf, Eric Herter, Carla and John Rensenbrink, Jean Sanborn and Lisa Tessler for their careful reading of my manuscript, for their insightful suggestions and unceasing encouragement to publish my memoirs.

Last, but not least, kudos to Matthew Bölken DeTroy for being the creative spirit behind the design of the book cover.

FOREWORD

Unpacking Intimate Memories:
Growing Up in the Third Reich

The title of Christine DeTroy's memoirs, *Remembering... Years of Hiding Behind Silence*, says it all. Growing up in the artists' colony of Worpswede in Northern Germany, not that far away from the city of Bremen, DeTroy was age four to seventeen when the Nazis were in power. This intimate memoir deals with her retrieval of her childhood memories some seventy years later.

The circular structure of the memoir is striking: it begins with DeTroy's moving account of her farewell visit to a Jewish grandmother, a neighbor, Frau Rosa Abraham, shortly before the older woman was to leave Worpswede and await her tragic fate as a victim of the Holocaust. The memoir concludes with the author's own present-day visit to Terezin, in the Czech Republic, the site of the Theresienstadt Concentration Camp where Frau Abraham was deported before her final deportation to the extermination camp of Treblinka. The memoir's circular structure lends a wholeness that reflects the authentic immediacy of DeTroy's voice.

Daily life in the Third Reich is portrayed in microcosm from the innocent perspective of a child emerging as a teen-ager. We meet not only the victim, Frau Abraham and her family, but the German bystanders of different political stripes of conformity: from those Nazi-party-members who like Christine's neighbor, serving as Nazi block spy on neighboring households, or a teacher who is buried in a Nazi flag to silent resisters like Christine's mother who takes her three daughters for a nature walk to avoid a Nazi-sponsored funeral that the citizenry is expected to attend. The circumspectness of the author's family of four women at mealtime is underscored by their avoidance of any political discussion in the presence of their housekeeper—who is the daughter of the above-mentioned block spy.

Christine's divorced parents provide a striking contrast in their markedly different reactions to the Nazi regime. Whereas Christine's mother was a professionally recognized landscape photographer, apolitical and therefore resistant to Nazi pressures, her father, trained as a lawyer, was in fact a designer of industrial lighting and stationed in Norway for part of the war—that his inventions and his activities were, in part, enlisted by the Nazi regime is alluded to by the author. Christine's non-conformist maternal grandmother with her stays in South America in the earlier decades of the twentieth century to aid the abject poor and as an adherent of a stringent vegetarian diet make her *the* iconoclastic figure of the book—an idealist, her indomitable spirit doubtlessly inspired her granddaughter-author. Like her grandmother, DeTroy was to become staunchly pacifist!

One of the most revelatory portions of the memoirs is DeTroy's moving account of the evacuation program which sent her along with her high-school classmates to southern Germany away from the repeated bombings in the North, to live for an extended period of time. This portion of the memoir concentrates on the warm-hearted education, both secular and religious, that the Northern

German Protestant girls were getting both from the Southern-German Bavarian nuns and from their new Protestant minister. Clearly, the spirituality that was being nurtured stood in marked contrast to the pseudo-religious and authoritarian indoctrination that these pupils had endured in their own schools at home.

Bonuses abound in this volume: beautifully reproduced evocative nature photographs done by DeTroy's mother and original documents ranging from the author's or close relatives' personal letters to sundry pieces of autobiographical writing. These documents anchor the memoir in an historical reality that is unique. This poignant memoir is, indeed, all of one piece!

Steven R. Cerf
Skolfield Professor Emeritus of German
Bowdoin College, Brunswick, Maine

Typical thatch-roofed home of a peat farmer on a foggy morning in the fall. Photo by Julie Meiners-Bölken (JMB). ca. 1940.

Remembering...

Years of Hiding Behind Silence

Abraham house on the Richtweg in Worpswede -- around 1930.

INTRODUCTION

My writing started fourteen years ago with an essay about my long-ago Jewish neighbor Frau Abraham, as part of my honors project at Bowdoin College entitled "Retrieving the Past: The Role of Memory and the Holocaust in the Novels of W.G. Sebald." The memory of my farewell visit with Frau Abraham in 1939, her disappearance from her home in Worpswede and the knowledge, although unconfirmed at that time, of her murder in a concentration camp was the primary motive to reach back into my childhood to retrieve the early experiences and impressions of the years under the Hitler regime and World War II. Slowly, with barren months and years in between, another followed this first essay and yet another, each addressing specific people and experiences as well as my reaction to the life that unfolded before my eyes so many years ago.

The essays don't follow a particular time sequence, instead they were written in response to my attempt to recount a series of events or to describe a particular person who had a significant influence on my life. My writing is a personal history of what I observed and felt during my childhood in Worpswede—a childhood simultaneously impacted by a loving family and good friends as well as the cruelty of injustice, war and dictatorship. Inevitably the essays contain duplications of people, of events and places recalled within a different context and with new insights. There may be inconsistencies in my perceptions, mirroring the changes and demands I faced in my attempt to reconstruct the past. The positioning of my recollections may appear like a pile of tiles, waiting to be incorporated into a coherent mosaic. In the same way each individual essay, seemingly positioned at random, attempts to lead to the whole of a particular period of my life. I hope that I have been able to achieve coherency.

Do I think that my history is important enough to share with others? This is a question a writer of memoirs inevitable has to ask herself throughout the process. Do I have a goal and what is it? Where am I going with my re-examination of the past? My answer? My intention is to be a witness—to give voice to the small and larger events of my youth during a larger-than-life history, the years of the Third Reich dominated by the Holocaust and World War II, especially for my children and grandchildren. An unexpected result of the retrieval and examination of my childhood has been that it has led to a process of self-discovery, a careful scrutiny of the self within the framework of events and people who impacted and shaped my ideas and actions to this day. For that I am thankful.

Another related question confronts me: why do I write? Will my observations raise questions among my readers? Will any of my questions lead to answers? My hope is that questions will be raised and in turn lead to reflect on what our role in our society is: am I a vocal witness, am I a bystander silenced by fear, am I a denier because someone else is doing my thinking for me? I don't believe that answers are as crucial as questions. I'm concerned that answers can lead to rigidity and self-righteousness, to a kind of dictatorship of the mind. We don't need dictatorship in any form whatsoever! Thus I champion questioning, not to avoid taking a stand on ethics and values, but for the sake of examining the conditions under which we live and how we respond to them. I champion questioning for the sake of knowing that we have choices, even if they may be limited or are difficult to make. I champion questioning for the sake of being able to admit that we may not always be able to live up to our expectations of ourselves. I write in order to gain clarity.

Brunswick, Maine—April 2015

Rosa Abraham (center) with her daughter Henny Goldschmidt and grandson Siegfried Goldschmidt in front of the Abraham house. ca. 1927.

REMEMBERING FRAU ABRAHAM

JULY 10, 2000

This letter by the author was written July 10, 2000
to the grandson of Frau Abraham

I am writing to you at the suggestion of Klaus-Peter Schulz of Osterholz-Scharmbeck (Germany), whom I recently met during a visit to my hometown of Worpswede. For some time I have been searching for relatives of Frau Abraham, a neighbor of my family for a few years when I was a little girl. I understand that you are her grandson. We may have met when I lived in the little house that sits back from the larger Abraham house on a small street that was originally called Richtweg. But I do not remember you. I believe my mother, Julie Meiners-Bölken, my two older sisters and I moved into the house in the early thirties, probably around 1932. I was four years old at the time. My family lived in the small house for about three or four years and then moved into an upstairs apartment in what had been an art gallery, owned by the Seekamp family. I believe Frau Seekamp was a friend of your grandmother's.

Although we were your grandmother's neighbors for those few years I hardly remember her except for her occasional walks in the garden. But I have one distinct memory of your grandmother—visiting her one Sunday afternoon with Frau Seekamp. It was in late fall of 1939—I had just turned eleven years old—when she asked me to accompany her to say good-bye to your grandmother. On the way over Frau Seekamp told me that your grandmother was to be deported to Poland, but I now understand that she moved to Bremen and lived with or near her sisters-in-law in Bremen before she was deported. The visit was subdued and somber; the two women spoke quietly and I don't think I heard anything of their conversation. Before Frau Seekamp and I left, the women asked me to play a piece on the piano. It was a very confusing and unsettling visit for me. I sensed the sadness and seriousness that lay heavily on us, but no one seemed to be able do anything about it. I never saw your grandmother again.

The memory of your grandmother has stayed with me all the many years since then and, although I was sure of her eventual fate, I have often wondered where her family was (years ago, I learned that she had relatives in New York City) and if anything more is known about her fate. Most recently I discussed this with one of my professors at Bowdoin College and he suggested that I put an ad in the *Aufbau*, a bi-monthly German-Jewish newspaper published in New York City. I followed his advice and received a reply from a Mr. Meyers of Middletown, CT, who had undertaken a search of his relatives, among them the early Abraham family in Worpswede. My next contact was a researcher in Bremervörde (Germany) and from there I was referred to Mr. Schulz who had done considerable research on Jewish families in and beyond Bremen.

In June of this year I visited Worpswede and met the wife of the current Lutheran pastor who told me that you and your family had visited Worpswede a few times during the late eighties and early nineties. By chance I also discovered the memorial plaque in the local church, honoring your grandmother and her two sisters-in-law, all of whom perished in the concentration camp Theresienstadt.

You may ask what has prompted my late inquiry into the life and death of your grandmother. My answer is that what happened in Germany during the thirties and forties remains on my mind, especially my connection with your grandmother, vague as it may be.

In recent years I have read many books—histories, biographies and novels—about the Holocaust. In each case it has been more than a book for me as I am faced with the reality of knowing what happened to her.

I hope you will forgive my intrusion into your life and memories, but if it is possible and not too painful for you I would like to hear from you and perhaps meet with you in the near future. As I have three grown sons living in Connecticut (about an hour's train ride from New York City) I regularly travel to the region and could combine it with a visit to you.

The memory of my last visit with Frau Abraham, distinct as it still seems to me today, has nonetheless been impacted by the passage of time and the new perceptions I have gained through the events and experiences of the past sixty years. Yet the vision of the quiet woman who was our neighbor for about four or five years has remained my singular connection to my childhood under the shadow of the Holocaust.

For a child of eleven, the farewell visit to Frau Abraham was a bewildering experience. Not only because of the somberness, not only because of the silence of Frau Seekamp and Frau Abraham, broken only by my piano playing, but because of the surrealism of the event. Here was a woman, a long-time resident of Worpswede, who had not committed a crime, yet was about to be taken away like a criminal, consigned to an unknown fate, while everyone in the village appeared as if paralyzed, apparently unable to make a move to halt the unraveling of her life. I recall asking Frau Seekamp on our way home how Frau Abraham would be able to survive in post-Blitzkrieg Poland, a country where, according to my imagination, all houses had been destroyed or were barely inhabitable. Were there any roofs on the houses? Was there any heat? Any shield from the oncoming Eastern winter? Where and how could she live? How could she keep warm with only a few warm clothes in the one suitcase she would be allowed to take on her journey East? In retrospect, it may appear childish that my predominant concern was Frau Abraham's physical comfort at her impending deportation to Poland, but I'm certain that I could not envision that her destination was a death camp.

Frau Seekamp, a small quiet woman, in stature much like Frau Abraham, could not answer any of my questions. Looking back, I realize that her silence was based on a lack of knowledge as well as the pain of helplessness. I didn't ask any other questions, such as why the adults in Worpswede could not or would not intervene on behalf of Frau Abraham for I quickly grasped that Frau Seekamp did not have any answers for me. It was probably the first time in my life that I sensed the full meaning of helplessness; not only the helplessness of a child but the helplessness of adults who would not speak up against injustice, because they were afraid for their own lives. Years later, after I had participated in a number of demonstrations in support of civil rights activities in Chicago, in the face of possible violence by helmeted and gun-carrying policemen, I wrote to my mother and asked her what would have happened if a crowd of sympathetic Worpswede residents had accompanied

Frau Abraham to the local railroad station when she was being deported to Poland—my assumption being that this was the point of departure of her deportation. Could Nazi officials have done anything against a crowd of supporters? Could she have been saved? I felt cruel asking these rhetorical questions which implied that I charged my mother with complicity and cowardice, for I knew that she had resisted the dicta of the Third Reich by raising my two older sisters and me to question authority, injustice, and nationalism. Yet those questions had to be asked, even after the many years, which had passed since Frau Abraham's forced removal from Worpswede. No, I did not expect an answer from my mother, because I was well aware that the vise of fear of violent retribution was firmly in place in Nazi Germany even before Frau Abraham was deported. Already in 1939 it was no surprise that the residents of Worpwede turned away from Frau Abraham and tried to hide their shame behind a curtain of silence.

The meager facts about the Abraham family that I was able to uncover during the past year, cannot do justice to the dimensions of their lives. Frau Abraham's generation is gone, as is the following generation. The memories of the generation born in the early 1920s are largely clouded and obscured by age and the wish to forget. There are only a few printed references available to visualize the life of the Abraham family in Worpswede. Thus imagination and conjecture will have to fill the large gaps that exist between fragments of historical data and the actual lives of the family. However, I now know that the Abraham family settled in Worpswede well before the middle of the nineteenth century. At one time the family opened a butcher shop in the large white house which still stands near the center of the village. In addition to being a butcher, the family patriarch, Michael Abraham, was a cattle dealer and owned several acres of grassland behind his house Am Richtweg.

Michael and his second wife, Julie, had six children, some of whom immigrated to the United States before the end of the nineteenth century. According to a newspaper report, one of his sons, Hermann, was a candidate for a council seat in Worpswede in 1919. The article stated that although he was Jewish, his candidacy was not considered unusual during the Weimar Republic.

Despite the first appearances of uniformed S.A. members (storm troopers) in the early 1930s and the events which brought Hitler to power in January of 1933, Frau Abraham, widow of Hermann Abraham since 1923, decided to stay in Worpswede. Most likely she believed that because the Abraham family had been well integrated into the community she would not be singled out by the Nazi regime. She also had friends who supported her and secretly provided her with groceries and other necessities that were officially denied her. I surmise that she believed she could survive the Third Reich. Her daughter Henny, who had immigrated to the United States in the mid-thirties, was not able to persuade her mother to follow her. I now know that this hopeful, yet disastrous attitude was not unusual among many older Jewish citizens of Germany.

By the mid-thirties, two of Michael Abraham's daughters, Merri and Sophie, both widowed and in their seventies, lived in the nearby city of Bremen. In the fall of 1939, Frau Abraham, then sixty-seven years old, joined them after having left Worpswede in secret. This information contradicts my memory of Frau Abraham's deportation to Poland in 1939. It is most likely that her sisters-in-law persuaded her to leave Worpswede around that time. Perhaps it was under the guise of her presumed deportation to Poland that she moved to Bremen, into the anonymity of a larger city, in order to be safer from the increased rate of deportations. However, within three years, Rosa Abraham, née Lösermann, Merri Leesser, née Abraham, and Sophie Schwabe, née Abraham, were deported and perished in Theresienstadt.

Rosa Abraham's only living descendant, her grandson Siegfried, left Worpswede for the United States in 1935 still lives in New York State with his wife and their three adult children. They are the great-grandchildren of Rosa and Hermann Abraham.

Worpswede, according to documents issued by the Cloister of Osterholz in 1218 was originally listed as a farming community consisting of a group of peat farmers who settled in the boggy area, just north of the village as early as the Middle Ages. Peat cutting continued to the north of Worpswede in an area called Teufelsmoor (Devil's Bog), until the early 1970s. The early documents further state that during the seventeenth century a group of eight farmers, not associated with peat cutting, settled along a road that eventually was given the name of Bauernreihe (Farmers Row)—a street that still exists close to the center of Worpswede.

The settlement continued to grow. Sometime during the mid-eighteenth century a Royal Moor Commissioner by the name of Jürgen Christian Findorff (1720-1792) was sent to the region to survey the land and communities that had sprung up around the village. While Findorff worked in the area, the regional prince decided that the growing community needed a church to "civilize the population." Findorff was chosen as designer and builder of the first church in Worpswede. It was built according to the guidelines of the King of Hannover, who specified that its interior must not include any un-necessary ornamentation. To this very day the Zionskirche, dedicated in 1759, remains as simple as originally designed—dark colors of the moor predominate in the interior of the church.

In 1884 several young painters transformed the farming community from its rural beginnings in the Middle Ages to an art colony. According to Worpswede's more recently recorded history, Fritz Mackensen, Hans am Ende, Otto Modersohn, Fritz Over-beck and Heinrich Vogeler formed the first group of artists who, imbued by German Romanticism, were drawn to Worpswede's landscape. Its dark moor and contrasting white birches that lined the roads and paths, its wide sky and magnificent clouds, its remoteness from cities and art academies, inspired the painters. The young artists were determined to paint directly from nature. In 1889 they decided to settle in Worpswede and founded an art colony—still known today as Künstlerdorf Worpswede. Painters as well as writers and sculptors continued to follow the founders. Among them Paula Moderson-Becker and Ottilie Reyländer; the poet Rainer Maria Rilke and the sculptor Clara Rilke Westhoff. The sculptor-painter-designer Bernard Hoetger arrived within a few years of its founding. During the nineteen-thirties and forties more artists settled in Worpswede. They were an unconventional group of women and men—free spirits, determined to express their individualism by painting and writing. Most of them were indifferent to politics, except for one remarkable man—the idealist, painter and designer Heinrich Vogeler. This man, deeply impacted by the violence of World War I, founded the commune Barken-hof (now an art gallery dedicated to the early work of the artist) soon after the war. It became home to a group of artists and their families in 1919. In the spirit of an idealized Communism, the families shared their lives and work on the large property, taking care of the spacious house and extensive gardens and supporting one another in their artistic expressions for several years.

The Worpswede of which I became aware in the mid-thirties had changed and grown since the founding of the art colony. Gone were the commune Barkenhof and its founder Heinrich Vogeler. He immigrated to Soviet Russia in the late 1920s. Hans am Ende was killed during World War I. Otto Modersohn had moved to the emerging artist colony of Fischerhude, a small community close to Worpswede. Fritz Overbeck died of a stroke in 1909. Only Fritz

Mackensen continued to live and paint in Worpswede. He died in 1953. Since the years of founding, the artist community had considerably increased and diversified—it now included writers and poets, potters, weavers, goldsmiths, designers and framers. For my sisters and me, Worpswede and its environment was a place of beauty; it was a center of creativity, independent thinking and acceptance. Although my mother was neither a painter nor a writer, her skill and artistry as a landscape photographer assured her a place in the circle of artists—they were our family. I believe that being part of an independent yet inclusive community was key to our emotional survival during the Nazi regime, which, by the mid-thirties, had intruded into everyone's life. Yet wasn't our independent spirit an illusion to which we clung silently during the years of Hitler's dictatorship, the years of persecution and murder of those who were called "the foreign element?"

Do I remember when I first heard about the persecution of Jews? I think it began by hearing about *Kristallnacht* (Crystal Night) from my mother. Trying to conceal the horror and fear in her subdued voice, my mother told our trusted neighbor, Frau Seekamp, what she had heard from her father about the rounding up of Jewish people and the destruction of synagogues and Jewish businesses in Bremen during the night of November 9, 1938. I know that I did not read a newspaper at that age, but fifty years later, when I visited Munich, I saw an exhibit of newspapers from 1938. Among them were pages of the *Völkischer Beobachter*, a well-known Nazi newspaper, which prominently featured photographs of Kristallnacht, along with commentary. Contrary to the denial voiced by many Germans after the war, these newspaper articles were proof that the adult population had to be aware of the increasing, government-sponsored violence toward Jewish people. Sometime after Kristallnacht the term concentration camp (KZ) entered

A group of Worpswede's children listening to the reading by Worpswede author Wilhelm Scharrelmann at his home. Charly, Angela and Christa Meiners on the far right.

my vocabulary, although I cannot say if I had a concrete vision of what a concentration camp was at that time—this information came to us during the years of World War II in fragments of whispered rumors, too horrible to absorb.

To this day it is difficult to comprehend to what extent the Nazi regime terrorized everyone. The terror began with an overwhelming sense of the immediate and ever-prevailing power of the Nazis. Added to that were the elements of fear and distrust, cultivated by the regime through the appointment of a cadre of "listeners" and "observers," the block wardens, who had a presence in even the smallest towns. Few people lived without a Kafkaesque angst that one could be charged with an unknown crime against the state, which would lead to one's certain destruction. Therefore, the strong urge to live and survive, at whatever cost, generated a nation of murderers, accomplices, spies, informants, and bystanders.

What about the artists in Worpswede and their commitment to individualism, independent thinking, and truth when the Third Reich intruded into their lives? I remember that a handful of artists became party members and outspoken Hitler supporters—among them Fritz Mackensen. While some of the local writers probably wrote articles about the glory of the Third Reich, they did not gain much of an audience. Likewise, several painters proclaimed the new Germany, but I don't recall seeing one painting displaying the swastika or other symbols of Nazism. However, the officialdom of the Nazi Party heralded the work of German artists, including the artists of Worpswede, whose work primarily focused on "man's connection to nature." It was considered "Germanic" art, as distinguished from foreign, "degenerate" art. Therefore, while the landscape paintings of the earliest Worpswede artists were lauded, the "primitive" paintings of Worpswede's best known artist, Paula Modersohn-Becker, as well as the works by other modern painters, were labeled "degenerate" and were summarily removed from art galleries throughout Germany.

Was there any resistance among the artists? I believe most of them retreated into an "inner resistance"—aware of the horror, but paralyzed by the enormity and extent of the Nazi party apparatus and not willing to countenance it. Therefore, most of the artists, in so far as was possible, turned away from the politics of the day and continued to focus their creativity on lyrical writing and painting. A commentary from a 1989 article in the *Worpswede Intern* refers to the fact that most of the artists had been apolitical for years and their retreat to their desks and easels did not signify a serious deviation from previous behavior. To a large extent Worpswede became a community of bystanders; people who privately agonized over their stance, but remained bystanders nonetheless. In retrospect, it appears to me that the only resistance that manifested itself in Worpswede was in private conversations, secret exchanges of "forbidden" information within the circle of artists who could trust each other. However, I recall the time when the painter Benny Huys was imprisoned in a penitentiary for the crime of having listened to a foreign radio station. Without hesitation his artist friends and others quietly rallied and shared their food with his wife and children. The family of a person convicted of a "crime against the State" was not entitled to ration cards.

Despite the fact that many artists and other villagers tried to shield themselves from becoming connected to the Nazi regime by quietly retreating into their own world, the control of the Party reached into the life of each resident. Eventually each artist, each tradesman and craftsman had to conform to a Nazi edict requiring membership in an organization under the jurisdiction of the Party. Since each adult was registered with the local police there was little chance that anyone would be overlooked, whether well-known or not. Within this context I remember the day when my mother received her summons for a state examination, which would lead to her official certification as a photographer and as a member of a

Women's League. When she returned from the examination in the county seat she confessed to her three daughters that she had failed the test. We were astounded as well as amused, because she was an accomplished landscape photographer and we didn't think there was anything about photography, including developing and printing, she did not know. However, the examining officer had neither checked her portfolio of photos nor her knowledge of her craft. Instead he tested her knowledge of Nazi history, such as the birthday of Hitler and other official data of which she knew nothing. Since this information was drummed into our heads in school on a continual basis we sat down with our mother and became her tutors. My mother, who had been our teacher and guide, leading us to an understanding and rejection of totalitarianism and Nazi philosophy, was now our student whom we had to teach the significant dates of the Hitler regime.

Recently, as I retrieved the memories of those years, this incident, which seemed so ludicrous at the time, took on a sinister aspect. I was assailed by the horror that we, although unwilling, nonetheless obeyed the decrees of the Third Reich for we believed that we had to obey the laws in order to protect our mother from incarceration. I admired my mother then and I admire her now for the strength and courage that she displayed in so many ways during the years of the Nazi regime. I admire her for her honesty in sharing her rejection and fears of the Nazis with us, trusting us with a knowledge which freed us, yet could put all of us in danger. I especially admire my mother for her courage on one particular day when she took us for a walk through the fields and woods surrounding Worpswede. It was the day of the funeral of one of our grade school teachers, a dedicated Nazi, who had requested that he be buried dressed in his Nazi uniform, boots and all, wrapped in the swastika flag. The funeral became an official event and the whole community of Worpswede was to be present. My mother's decision to take a walk in the countryside with us, away from the funeral ceremony, impressed me very much. Perhaps it was only a small token of resistance, but for me it was a significant symbol of her independent thinking and action.

The years of the Hitler regime were years of fear for children and adults alike. No matter where you were, on the street, in a store, or in school, you felt insecure, because you were never sure if you were being watched doing something punishable. Most of all I remember my ever-present fear that our mother would be taken from us if my sisters or I accidentally made a remark that could be interpreted as anti-Nazi. With the start of World War II, our insecurity and fear increased, especially after the air raids began. Many a night, when the nearby city of Bremen was bombed and the planes circled above Worpswede, we had to rush down into our basement in order to seek cover. Yet it was nothing when I consider the fate of the people who were deported into concentration camps. No one in our immediate family was persecuted, no one was incarcerated; not one member of my extended family was tortured or murdered. Our home was not confiscated. My sisters and I were allowed to go to school. We didn't have much to eat, but we ate on a regular basis. During the winter our apartment was cold due to the coal shortage, but we never froze. The simple reality was this: not being Jewish, we did not have to fear selection for deportation or destruction. The knowledge of being privileged because of my birth lies heavily on me. As a survivor I am relieved that I was able to escape death. However, when this escape is at the cost of another person's life, it is a dilemma that remains unresolved.

What about Siegfried Goldschmidt's youth in Worpswede? What kind of memories was he able to retrieve when he revisited Worpswede during the winters of the late eighties and in 1991? The series of extraordinary circumstances that led me to the search for relatives of Frau Abraham eventually led to partial answers to those questions. My inquiry into the whereabouts of possible Abraham descendents in the United States that began with a search ad in the April 20, 2000 edition (ironically the date of Hitler's birthday) of the newspaper *Aufbau*, led to a correspondence with Arthur Meyers, great-grandson of Michael Abraham, now living in Connecticut. Based on research of his ancestors in Germany—he included a copy of the Abraham family tree—I was able to confirm that the family had indeed lived in Worpswede on the small dirt road named *Am Richtweg*. It was a powerful moment for me when I received his letter and realized that my veiled memories of Frau Abraham were indeed based on fact. In my hands I held written proof that Frau Abraham had lived in Worpswede and that she had been our neighbor. However, at that time I did not know which of the women's names cited on the pages was *my* Frau Abraham—she was only known to me as Frau Abraham.

With Mr. Meyers' information in hand I visited Worpswede in June of 2000 and continued my research of the Abraham family. I found only a few people of my generation who remembered anything about the family; still fewer wanted to talk about the events that happened six decades ago. However, in my conversations with Klaus-Peter Schulz, an unofficial researcher of former Jewish families of the greater Bremen area, I was able to gather additional information about the Abraham family. I learned that Frau Abraham's first name had been Rosa, that she had married into the Abraham family and that she had had two children. I discovered that her daughter Henny and her grandson Siegfried had immigrated to the United States in 1934 and 1935 respectively. Siegfried's name was changed to Frederick, Fred for short, in 1942, prior to his being sent overseas with his U.S. Army unit. He and his family now live in New York State. Before I left his office, Mr. Schulz directed me to the Lutheran pastor in Worpswede for further information. It was the pastor's wife who gave me her impressions on meeting Fred during the latter's visits to Worpswede in the late eighties and early nineties. Her most vivid memory of Fred, confirmed by Mr. Schulz and another Worpswede resident, focused on his evident happiness during the first couple of days of his visit to his childhood home. However, his high spirits would soon change into expressions of anger about the past, startling old schoolmates and others, who had assumed that the past they had buried had also been silenced by him. Their surprise at his outbursts confirmed what I had slowly gleaned from my conversations in Germany: a confirmation of the wide gulf that continues to exist between the Holocaust memories of the residents of Germany and the victims of Nazi persecution. Is it possible, in addition to an intentional silencing of the memories of the past, that the distance of time and the demands of daily life in Germany since 1945 have obscured and superseded the events of those years for most residents?

While on a morning's walk in late June of 2000, leading me to a visit of Worpswede's Lutheran church, I was startled to discover a large memorial plaque inside the building. In Gothic letters, carved into a large plank of finished oak, were the names of Rosa Abraham, Mary Leeser, and Sophie Schwabe, the years and places of their birth and the simple, but grief-filled words: "Died in Theresienstadt." I trembled at this sudden confrontation with the tangible, incontrovertible proof that Frau Abraham and her sisters-in-law had been murdered in a concentration camp. Here was the concrete evidence for which I had not been prepared despite my presentiments. My mourning for the women was increased by the knowledge that no one in Worpswede had told me about the memorial plaque. How was that possible? Wasn't it well known that this plaque existed? Is the silence about the memorial the ever-present symbol of striving for erasure of the Nazi past? A few days later I was told that it was Fred Goldschmidt who had commissioned the local artist and designer,

Hans-Georg Müller, grandson of the idealist Heinrich Vogeler, to carve the plaque in 1991. The memorial presented to the local church in the early nineties—there is no synagogue in Worpswede—is a stark reminder of the three innocent women who were abandoned during the Holocaust. Yet, does anybody take time to remember them?

During Fred Goldschmidt's occasional post-war visits in Worpswede the regional press frequently interviewed him. In his interviews he gave voice to the memories of his youth in Worpswede, the community that Fred had loved as a young boy but learned to distrust and hate by the time he was twelve. He clearly remembered the name-calling: *"Jude, Jude, Jude"* (Jew, Jew, Jew) by his schoolmates and the painful recognition that his former friends had become enemies. Despite the traumatic memories of being chased and taunted; despite the bitter knowledge of his grandmother's and his aunts' murder during the Third Reich, Fred was nonetheless drawn to revisit his earliest home. In one interview, he expressed the conflicting emotions engendered by confronting the memories of his years in Worpswede: "This is where I experienced my childhood, that's why I return" and "You know what makes me crazy? This is where my youth was destroyed."

The newspaper interviews afford insight into the life of the Abraham family that for years was the only Jewish family permanently residing in Worpswede. Fred's recollections, stemming from the late twenties, document the isolation and exclusion the family suffered as open anti-Semitism began to be encouraged throughout Germany. In the 1920s, the butcher shop of his great-grandfather had given way to a dry goods store, managed by his father, Julius Goldschmidt. Fred remembers the original success of his father's store and the fact that his family was the first to purchase a brand new car every other year. However, because of the increasing effect of boycotts on Jewish stores, the dry goods store was closed even before Hitler came to power. By then Fred's parents had separated and his father immigrated to South Africa.

Additional details of Fred's childhood and youth were revealed to me when I was welcomed into the home of the Goldschmidt family in October of 2000. It was an afternoon of trying to reach back to Fred's years in Worpswede, but there were few words. The immediacy of my presence as a former resident of Worpswede was an inevitable barrier to a free and open conversation between us. In the course of the afternoon we established that he did not remember the three little girls who moved into the small house in back of his grandmother's home, probably about three years before Fred left for New York City, just as I did not remember the teenager as my neighbor. But perhaps we instinctively shielded ourselves from a possible common memory.

Fred shared photographs of his grandmother with me and I finally saw the face of Frau Abraham again, a face I had tried to visualize for many years without success. Suddenly, as I looked at the small black and white snapshot, I recalled the person, the small, quiet woman who always dressed in black. I recalled seeing her sometimes outside the laundry room in the rear of her house or in the back yard. I have a vision of her in her black coat, walking towards the bakery, Bäckerei Kück, less than a block from our homes. I think that I remember her wearing the yellow star, but I am wrong. Research has confirmed that the Nazi edict requiring Jews to wear the identifying Star of David was not put into effect until September of 1941. Fred showed me a snapshot of his grandmother's living room, with the table and chairs in the center, and the door, which leads to the stairs—and suddenly I remembered the room where I had visited her with Frau Seekamp. The photos led to further fragments of memory—they, in turn, connected to real experiences, to memories, which I never expected to have confirmed. Among the photographs is a picture of the interior of the Lutheran church where the memorial plaque, honoring the memory of his grandmother and aunts, is located. High above the altar hangs a large golden star. Within its oval center the word *Yahwe* is written in Hebrew letters. During the ceremonial presentation of the Abraham memorial plaque to the minister of the church, Fred remembers saying: "If the Hebrew word for God is displayed in your church, the church should not deny Jews." I can recall this star from my youth. However, I don't recall the word Yahwe. Was it covered up during the Nazi period? No one in Worpswede was able to tell me when the word Yahwe reappeared.

Both Fred and I grew up in Worpswede, we were even neighbors for a few years. Shouldn't those simple facts assure similar memories? Fred's memories are overshadowed by the political events of the Third Reich; events, which robbed him of his childhood and subjected him and his family to harassment and isolation. Eventually they led to the loss of his family and home while only a teenager. My recollections include, despite fear and insecurity during the Nazi years, a protected childhood. However, among my childhood memories the farewell visit to Frau Abraham continues to stand out. This visit not only epitomizes the trauma of the Nazi years but also remains a most profound experience. Although more than six decades have passed since the visit, it continues to raise many questions. Memories of the visit retrieve the questions of a child, who was not able to understand the actions and events of her immediate surroundings. These questions have now shifted to the adult, who, despite increased knowledge and the ability to analyze past events, still cannot find convincing answers. Why did Worpswede abandon Frau Abraham, the woman whose fate remains a symbol of the millions of Jews who were persecuted and murdered? Was it because of anti-Semitism and belief in the Nazi tenets? Was it indifference and apathy? Was fear of the consequences of opposing the laws of the Third Reich, even in a small village like Worpswede, the force that led to moral paralysis?

Despite the memorial plaque in the church, a visual reminder of the Holocaust, the residents of Worpswede remain silent. They want to forget. In my recent correspondence with former schoolmates I have received some support for my search, but there has also been reluctance to re-enter the past. While pursuing a lead to connect with an older resident who had some personal memories of Frau Abraham, I was recently asked by a mutual acquaintance to cease my questioning. The woman, now eighty-eight years old, asked to be relieved from re-visiting the past. She didn't want to speak about the Hitler years anymore. "Too many years have passed. No one wants to remember that time."

In other letters from childhood friends I have sensed the unspoken charge that I do not have the right to retrieve the old memories relating to the Holocaust and Worpswede's posture during the Hitler regime. The charge points toward my having left Germany two years after the war and, living in the United States since 1947, having been spared most of the post-war years of hunger, self-accusation, and the shame of being German. I am well aware that my experiences in the U.S. haven't been comparable, especially since I was seldom scrutinized and judged on the basis of my origin. However, despite living in a different world, I have tried to reassure my friends that the physical separation from Germany has never separated me from the common responsibility for the Holocaust. Not only that, but the events of the Third Reich and Frau Abraham's abandonment and murder continue to influence the direction of my life to this day. Knowing that I never wanted to avert my eyes to injustice, that I never wanted to wait until fear would paralyze me and coerce me into becoming a bystander, I chose to be a human rights activist after I arrived in this country. The connection to Frau Abraham, established sometime during the early 1930s when a little girl was a neighbor of this quiet older woman, remains unbroken.

"WHAT DOES WAR FEEL LIKE?"

"All war is ultimately a war against civilians and children."
—Unknown

"What does war feel like?" This was the question I asked Mami, our mother, on Sunday afternoon, August 27, 1939, as she, my two older sisters Charly and Angela and I were standing in our living room. A few minutes earlier the door bell had rung in our apartment and a uniformed member of the *Sturm Abteilung* (S.A.) "storm trooper", thrusting the Nazi salute into our faces, had handed my mother a handful of printed sheets, which, according to his explanation, were ration cards—*Lebensmittelkarten*. The S.A. man left promptly after this delivery, his arm slicing the air with a repeat performance of "Heil Hitler." Mami turned ashen. Quietly she told us that the arrival of the ration cards confirmed her fears that a war would soon break out. Hence my question to Mami: "What does war feel like?"

I knew that Mami had lived through a war. She was nearly eleven years old when World War I began in August of 1914, close to my age on this Sunday in late August, and I was sure she would remember some of her feelings. However, except for a shrug of her shoulders and an expression of apprehension on her face, Mami did not respond. I wanted to ask her if we would experience a distinct feeling the moment war started and if our small world of Worpswede, the artists' colony in northern Germany, would change with the onset of war. But Mami's facial expression made it clear that this was not a time for speculation and explanation. For the time being the ration cards, the reason for the somber mood in our home, remained untouched on the buffet in the living room. Silently Mami went into her office; my sisters and I went into our rooms.

As I revisit this scene, I am not only reminded of the moment when the delivery of ration cards ushered a sense of unease into our home, but it also brings back the sound of a uniformed S.A. man stomping up the stairs to our apartment, the harshly expressed Heil Hitler and the outstretched, up-thrust arm. This was not a greeting, but rather like a corporeal threat from which one wanted to retreat.

We received frequent visits from the S.A. shortly before and during the war. They generally occurred on Sundays. Why did they choose to intrude into the privacy of our home—and the homes of other Worpswede residents—on that specific day? From a practical viewpoint it was likely the time when the S.A. would find most families at home. Yet, the psychological impact of disrupting a quiet Sunday by a uniformed messenger of the government may have been a calculated consideration. Collections for one or another Nazi cause were generally the reason for a visit by a member of the S.A. Among them was the *Eintopf* collection, based on the Nazi edict that each family had to cook a "one-pot" meal one Sunday per month. The money saved by cooking this simple meal had to be donated to a designated Nazi program.

The S.A. also delivered official announcements to each home after the small weekly newspaper, *Worpsweder Wochenblatt,* was shut down. It was on April 12, 1939 that the editor and publisher of the local paper, Hugo Domreis, informed his readers that permission to publish official community notices in his weekly newspaper had been withdrawn by county authorities. Therefore, without the income from the ads, he was financially unable to continue publication of the paper. The brevity of this sober announcement pointed toward a much more complicated, political explanation to eliminate the *Worpsweder Wochenblatt*. The Nazi machine was very efficient in erasing community voices.

I keep returning to my original question: "What does war feel like?" as I try to reconstruct my first impressions of World War II. The news of Germany's invasion of Poland on Friday, September 1, 1939, intruded into our home with a series of radio reports on the destruction of hundreds of Polish planes and tanks by the German Air Force. Our little radio, sitting on a low shelf in a built-in cabinet in the living room, mechanically gave the daily count of the destruction inflicted upon Poland. Over the weekend, one report after the other spoke of a succession of victories by the German military over the Polish armed forces, of Polish soldiers who laid down their arms and were taken prisoner, and of Polish cities and towns that were destroyed by heavy bombing. The word *Blitzkrieg* was coined because of the lightening speed with which German troops conquered Poland. What was my response to all of this? I recall my disbelief, because it was impossible to comprehend the extent and rapidity of the reported destruction. Since the reports focused on the devastation of Polish war materiels by German planes, it seemed to me that the war was one of machines versus machines. Throughout the brief war German casualties were hardly mentioned in the radio reports. A little over four weeks later Poland capitulated. Was the war over?

Aside from compliance with the strict orders for black-out, backed up by threats of jail sentences, I don't recall any significant changes in our home and lives during the first few months of World War II. However, although school and life at home continued at its usual pace, I remember living with an increasing sense of foreboding as if waiting in silence for something terrible to happen, something that no one could prevent. My sisters and I, as well as our closest friends, had been used to keeping political comments to ourselves for some time, but with the start of the war all of us became much more conscious of the need to be cautious in our conversations. It became known that political vigilance by official listeners and informers—block wardens (*Blockleiter*)—was increasing. I recall the day when Frau Seekamp, our trusted downstairs neighbor, quietly told me to "be careful what you talk about during your dinner time when your housekeeper is present." Although this advice was given to me in an offhand manner, I understood the importance of what she had said and immediately repeated her words to Mami. Within a few days my mother discovered that the father of our housekeeper Lina, affectionately called Linchen by us, had become a block warden. As such, he would naturally rely on his daughter to assist him in gathering information on the people she was in touch with. From then on our mealtime conversations revolved around the more mundane events of our daily lives, such as the weather, my mother's photographic assignments, school, and our garden. In addition to the awkwardness around the dinner table it was very uncomfortable to have to distrust Linchen, for she had been a part of our family for some time. Not only did she preside over our household, but when my mother was out-of-town on assignments, she also took on the parenting role. Had Linchen ever reported our conversations? My sisters and I didn't want to believe that she could have betrayed us, because we were very fond of her. Yet, while the trusting relationship between Linchen and us had to change, it was never completely severed. However, I never visited her father, Vater Böse, the cabinet-maker, again. Previously, I had frequently walked to his one-man shop and watched him work. I loved the smell of fresh wood and I felt comfortable and accepted in his workshop. I remember the day he built a coffin. As he was sanding the finished coffin I wanted to ask if it frightened him to think of the corpse that would be put into the coffin, but since we seldom talked I didn't dare to initiate a conversation, especially not on the topic of death.

As I remember my visits to the workshop of this quiet man I ask myself: what happened to Vater Böse that would make him a Blockleiter? Was it possible that this ordinary man had become a convinced Nazi? Had he been lured by the notion of being sought out as a "trusted" citizen by officialdom although the block warden was the lowest position in the Party's organizational pyramid? Had he been afraid to refuse the appointment to Blockleiter, fearing harm for himself and his family? Despite my attempts to consider a number of excuses for his decision to accept the appointment as block warden, I know that Vater Böse, willingly or unwillingly, had become one of the many minor functionaries on whom the success of Nazi control depended.

The creation of the position of Blockleiter was an obvious consequence of war, a tool to heighten distrust among neighbors and friends. I believe that from the day Hitler was elected chancellor of Germany, his totalitarian regime encouraged suspicion among all people in order to subvert any possible resistance. Fear of the stranger was encouraged. Informing on the stranger, as well as on a neighbor, was encouraged. In this context I was very puzzled by a sixth-grade reading assignment given to our class shortly after the war with Russia had begun. The story was about a family in the Soviet Union whose children had reported their parents' anti-communist conversations to the local police, leading to the arrest and deportation of the parents. This story of manipulation, pitting children against their parents and encouraging them to betray their mothers and fathers, was to remind us of the terror of Communism and its infiltration into the sanctity of a family. But wasn't the same message impressed onto the minds of German children? Betrayal for the good of the nation, especially after a couple of years into World War II, began to be considered an act of patriotism. Vater Böse and his daughter Linchen, minor players in the Nazi game, were two people caught in the web of sanctioned betrayal.

Linchen was typical of the daughters of farmers, craftsmen, and shopkeepers in Worpswede. Raised in a modest home, she finished the required eight years of public schooling, was confirmed in the Lutheran church and at age fifteen went to work as a *Mädchen,* a domestic apprentice, in order to learn to cook and clean, to set a proper table, and acquire middle-class manners. I believe Linchen started to work in our home when she was nearly nineteen years old. My sisters and I became very fond of her; she was kind and gentle, seldom cross. This made it all the more difficult for our whole family when we had to distance ourselves from her because of politics.

I remember meeting Linchen's future husband, Friedel, before they were engaged. He was a soldier and loved motorcycles; later on I found out that he was an enthusiastic Nazi. Although our relationship with Linchen had changed due to her father's Nazi post, Mami, my sisters, and I stayed in touch with her after she left to marry Friedel. We remained her *Meiners Kinder* just as she remained "our" Linchen, a person who, we insisted, existed separately from her Blockleiter father and her Nazi husband. Today, more than ever, I am aware of the contradictions on which our relationship with Linchen was based and my reflections confirm that we were not always willing to let personal ties be torn apart by politics.

Although I have traveled to Germany infrequently since 1947, I have always stopped at Linchen's each time I visited Worpswede. Whenever I arrived at her doorstep she greeted me with joy. We would talk about our lives and exchange photos of our children, and eventually our grandchildren, over a cup of tea and a piece of cake. Her husband usually stayed in the background. It was only during a visit in the summer of 2000, after Friedel had died and Linchen was eighty-two years old, that I had a chance to talk with her about the Nazi years in connection with my research on our former neighbor, Frau Abraham. Linchen spoke very hesitantly about her few memories of Frau Abraham, but those few sentences led to an impulsive explanation, as if to justify her and her husband's previous feelings about Hitler: "He made us feel that we counted for something," she burst out. "You know, being a Mädchen was the lowest position you could have. Even though Mami, you, and your sisters, treated me well and made me feel appreciated, that could not change that fact." Linchen went on to tell me about a couple of motorcycle trips she and Friedel had been able to take at no cost through the Nazi program *Kraft durch Freude* (strength through joy). "We could go on vacation and stay in hotels; we were respected." Our conversation ended with an apologetic, defensive comment about not knowing about the horror of the Holocaust. "Friedel didn't know about it either." Her daughter, Renate, who, along with her husband, stopped by during our conversation, was surprised to hear her mother speak about her memories of the Nazi years. Never before had she shared this information with her daughter. As Renate asked her mother more questions Linchen withdrew into herself and did not want to speak about her memories anymore. We parted in tears. Linchen died in the summer of 2001.

What did war feel like? The painful reality of the Hitler regime and World War II, a war silenced for a few months after the *Blitzkrieg* in Poland, was brought home to me during a last visit to Frau Abraham. On a dreary Sunday in November of 1939, when our downstairs neighbor, Frau Seekamp, asked me to accompany her on a farewell visit to her friend who was about to be deported to Poland. To my knowledge, Frau Abraham's disappearance was never publicly acknowledged. Was her name ever mentioned again in the living rooms of Worpswede?

How was it possible that Hitler's march across Europe was not stopped? The first country to fall was Poland; after that the *Wehrmacht* occupied Scandinavia; then Holland and Belgium. I don't recall hearing much about military opposition until Germany invaded France. The words "Maginot Line" remain imprinted on my mind. It was said that it was France's most heavily fortified line of defense and would certainly stop the German army. A few weeks later radio broadcasts reported that the French defenses had been overrun without much fighting. Was it true or was it propaganda? Would the war be over soon or would Hitler continue his march into other countries? It appeared as if war between Germany and one or another European country became the norm.

However, Germany's military invasion of Russia engendered a shock among the German population. The news of the start of the Russian campaign reached us on a Sunday morning in late June of 1941. I remember that it was a singularly beautiful summer morning. After breakfast my sisters and I went into the common garden behind Haus Seekamp. The garden, which was reached by a short path, ran parallel to the rear apartment where the portrait painter Agnes Sander-Plump lived. Everyone knew her as Plumpchen, a gregarious and successful painter in her mid-fifties, a woman of great imagination and a fine sense of humor. Plumpchen had three grown children, two daughters and a son. We knew that her son, the aspiring painter Jochen, had been drafted into the army in 1940 and was stationed in France.

Seeing Plumpchen by an open window we greeted her with a *Guten Morgen* and asked, "Have you heard that Germany invaded Russia early this morning?" The color drained from her face and she looked frightened, as if ready to cry. What was wrong? With fear in her voice she told us that Jochen had been transferred to the Eastern front only a couple of weeks earlier and now she knew the reason— Jochen would be in the forefront of the invasion of Russia. The day turned bleak for Plumpchen and for all of us. For my sisters and me the news of the Russian invasion had not seemed any different than the other broadcasts of Germany's march across Europe. However, with Plumpchen's fear and dread so evident we became conscious of what war with Russia meant to her and, in turn, to us. Within a year Plumpchen received the news that Jochen was missing in action. Although she continued to hope that he would be found alive, even years after the war, he never returned.

Sometime after the end of the World War II, Plumpchen wrote and illustrated a book *Das Geheimnis der Kinder* (The Children's Secret), which was her loving memorial to Jochen, testifying to her never-lost hope that he might still be alive, living in some remote corner of the world. It is the story of two fatherless children and a dwarf who grants them a wish. Their wish is that they will find their father. Traveling across the world, the children, magically changed into dwarves, are either assisted or detained by various animals during their perilous journey in search of their father. The happy ending brings their father home. This book, tattered from years of reading it to my children, is still on my bookshelf and I realize how profoundly moving the story remains, as wars still tear sons and fathers, as well as daughters and mothers, away from their families. Plumpchen's memorial to Jochen, to all victims of war, to parents and children, needs to be translated and shared.

In contrast to the triumphant radio reports on the victories of the German army, the rows of silent wreaths in memory of Worpswede's fallen soldiers hung in the upper reaches of the sanctuary walls of the local Lutheran church, told a different story. Their story was about death, not about victory. By the early winter of 1939 there were only a few wreaths, but as the war went on, especially after the invasion of Russia, the wreaths began to cover both sides of the sanctuary walls, crowding each other. Ever increasing numbers of young and older women could be seen wearing black clothes—women with

closed, serious faces who silently mourned their husbands and sons.
I remember the family of Görge Spervogel, a young writer, who
died at the Russian front in the winter of 1943. His wife, Ellida, and
their two young children, Till and Göntje, had moved into the rear
apartment of *Haus Seekamp* after Plumpchen had moved away. I am
suddenly struck by the startling coincidence that both residents of
the apartment lost loved ones, young and promising artists, on the
Russian front. Till, Göntje and I, although the children were several
years younger than I, spent a lot of time together. I often took care of
them. The evening after the news of their father's death had reached
us I went to see the children. They were already in their beds but
too excited by the unfamiliarity of being at the center of an event to
go to sleep. Neither Till nor Göntje understood what had happened
to their father. Never to see him again was not a concept they could
understand. For that matter, I was as confused as they were. I don't
recall that Görge's death was spoken of often. Was it to spare the
children? I believe mothers internalized their pain and sorrow and
discouraged their children's questions about war and death, because
it was well known that the Nazi regime did not encourage expressions of personal grief and sadness. The death of a soldier was to be
looked upon as a heroic fulfillment of one's duty to the fatherland.
Any other interpretation was considered synonymous with betrayal.
Silence was the order of the day.

The memory of silence, hiding truth, sadness, and fear, retains its
impact on me to this day. However, I believe that we lived with two
kinds of silences—the silence born out of fear and the silence that
bolstered inner resistance. We adhered to the silence born out of fear
in order to survive physically. Its message was: "don't ask wrong
questions; don't give wrong answers." However, the silence generated
by inner resistance provided us with a kind of shield behind which
we were whole people. As children we felt brave and strong when

we chose not to say Heil Hitler upon entering or leaving a store. My girlfriend Barbara and I felt liberated on the day when we chose not to repeat the words of a Hitler Youth oath during an official ceremony, but instead moved our lips soundlessly. Silence protected our thoughts. Silence was on our minds when family and friends whispered fragments of information about the brutality of the Hitler regime to each other. Silence was the watchword when we pressed our ears close to our radio, now placed on a pillow so that the sound could not travel, as we listened to forbidden BBC news reports. Sharing "rumors" about the war and the regime and listening to a foreign radio station were two crimes punishable with incarceration in a penitentiary or concentration camp; there were times when these "crimes" led to death. Silence enabled us to survive—but I, as a child, did not think about the price of our survival.

As the war continued our stomachs grumbled more, especially during the winter, when gardens and fruit trees could not augment the shrinking rations. Ration cards were cut each year; coal and peat deliveries were limited; the stores were emptier. If there were complaints about the lack of food, they were quietly expressed among family members, certainly never in public. When food shortages became more obvious, a number of official efforts to reassure the populace that the Führer cared about "his people," were instituted. I remember days in late summer, after the rye and oat harvest had been brought in by local farmers, that groups of school children were sent into the fields in order to pick up individual ears of grain, which had been overlooked by the harvesters. Did we fill enough sacks to make it worthwhile and where were the sacks sent? Did it really help lessen anyone's hunger? Even as children we were quite cynical and believed that our gathering of grain was one of the meaningless "war efforts" contrived to convince everyone of the need for personal sacrifice. Every public action and program had political overtones. Each was created as a diversion, a visible demonstration of the government's "concern" for the *Volk*.

Another program, involving the labor of children, was the collection of horse chestnuts in the fall. We were outfitted with rakes and jute bags and gathered thousands of chestnuts, which had fallen off the horse chestnut trees around our homes. They were to be chopped up and distributed to local farmers, as an additive to pig feed. A later initiative focused on the raising of silk worms in each home in order to produce silk for parachutes. This idea did not go beyond the talking stage in Worpswede; not only because the cold climate of northern Germany was not conducive to growing mulberry trees, but most residents, primarily the farmers, quietly ridiculed the farfetched ideas of city folk.

During the war with Russia, in the winter of 1943, an order for donations of skis and ski poles was broadcast in Worpswede. Skis were going to be collected, painted white and shipped to the snowbound infantry in Russia. Due to a number of hills around Worpswede skiing was a popular sport in our village and a number of adults and children owned skis. Within a matter of a few days all our skis, except for the smallest sizes, had to be delivered to a warehouse in the next town. Sometime in the summer of 1945, months after the end of World War II, the skis were found in the exact same place—they had never made it to Russia. Had this order been based on a genuine need of soldiers caught in the Russian winter or had it been another propaganda ploy?

I have often wondered whether it was Nazism or the war that impacted me most during the years of 1939 to 1945? In retrospect I believe that they were parallel realities that often blended into one entity for me. The major difference between no-war and war seemed to be an increase in political strictures, along with the effect of air raids and the inadequacy of food rations. My fear of Nazis and the inevitable repercussions of "wrong" behavior or actions had been in place since before the war and continued unabated, if not height-ened, after the war with Poland began. Ever since I can remember I suffered from a sense of dread that our mother would be taken from us, deported, I assumed, if my sisters or I behaved contrary to Nazi rules. This anxiety led to some strange and, in retrospect, comical behavior of mine. With the beginning of the fifth grade, I attended a small private school in Worpswede. The building was divided into three rooms—one large classroom for the combined fifth and sixth grades on the left of the simple wooden building; a small room for the seventh grade in the center; and another large classroom for the combined eighth and ninth grades on the right. One day, when I was in the seventh grade, it was my assignment to sweep our classroom. As the principal (also Worpswede's mayor and its most dedicated Nazi) was watching me, I became very conscious of having to do an expert job with the broom. I don't think I had often swept at home and I was fearful that I would push the sand and dust around the class-room without being able to gather it into a pile and into the dustpan. Suddenly it seemed like a political test. I knew that I had to prove myself as a "diligent German girl," brought up by my mother to be a productive member of society. I was sure that this image would have to include knowing how to sweep carefully and skillfully. I still see myself trying to sweep calmly and efficiently, acting as though this was something I did every day, while I was inwardly shaking. Eventually the dust balls and sand ended up on the dustpan and our family was saved.

Life in Worpswede, far from the war zone, seemed to experience few visible changes during the first couple of years of the war. More than anything, I remember the continued presence of the ration cards, because of their impact on our meals. The memory of food scarcity brings the bakery next door, *Bäckerei Reiners*, to mind. Before the war, after our move to Haus Seekamp, my sisters and I visited the store at least once a week to buy a sweet roll with our allowance. After I became better acquainted with the baker, Vater Reiners, and his daughter Sina, I started to visit the family and the bakery on a regular basis. I recollect being fascinated by the large machine, shaped like an open kettle, in which the bread dough was stirred. I watched the bakers shape the dough into loaves on large floured tables and prepare the sheets of cake before they were pushed into the large oven. When I was around twelve years old I was allowed to help brush water on the loaves after they came out of the oven. I also trimmed the edges of large sheets of apple and plum cakes when they were done. The edges, being a little hard and sometimes burnt, were mine for the taking. A year later I helped glue the small pieces of ration cards—one for each loaf of bread sold—on large sheets of paper. I assume that the bakery received their rations of flour and other baking ingredients on the basis of the returned coupons. Everything was controlled by the State.

Vater Reiners, a large and quiet man, always with a kind expression on his face, headed up a family which included his wife, who was frequently ill, their daughter Sina, and their son Albert. Although a member of the Nazi party, Vater Reiners was an unusual man who saved, or at least improved, the lives of many people. Quietly, even though at risk of punishment by incarceration, he would put a loaf of bread into the hands of a person who had run out of ration cards, yet still had hungry mouths to feed before the next month's issue of *Brotkarten*. I remember my father visiting us in Worpswede a few times each year—my father, who had looked well-fed at the beginning of the war, had become haggard as the years went on. At the end of each visit he would stop at *Bäckerei Reiners* and be given one or two loaves of bread to take home to his new family in Berlin. Vater Reiners was a unique and compassionate man. Saying goodbye to him before I left for the United States in June of 1947 was very painful. I remember the warm embrace, our exchange of a hoped for *Auf Wiedersehen,* while we both knew that we might never see each other again. Vater Reiners must have been nearly seventy years old when I left and he was not well.

Along with my memories of Vater Reiners I also remember his grown children, Sina and Albert. Sina was the oldest and worked in the store along with helping her mother keep house. There was also a large garden and a few pigs that needed taking care of. Sina was very much like her father, friendly and accepting; quietly going about her work, and making me feel welcome in her kitchen. My first memory of Albert is seeing him in the yellow/brown S.A. uniform, with the dark brown leather strap coming diagonally across his wide chest, as he stood in front of his father's bakery. Did he participate in the random violence of the storm troopers? Where? I don't know and I pray that he never did. After the war started Albert could be seen in the grey/green uniform of the German army when he came home on leave. I saw more of Albert after he came home from the war, sometime during 1945. The war had aged him and he seemed subdued. Within a matter of days he returned to his work in the bakery and gradually took on the major share of the work. Many years later, Albert, then in his sixties, was elected and re-elected mayor of Worpswede. I know that Albert had gone through the de-nazification process right after the war and it had been established that, aside from having been a member of the S.A. for a few years, he had never held a Nazi post. It was his reputation for being a thoughtful and dependable person, that earned him the mayoralty in Worpswede. Although I personally liked Albert very much, I was surprised that a former S.A. member could be considered for the office of mayor.

Reflecting on my friendship with the Reiners family forces me not only to face Albert's S.A. past, but also his father's membership in the Nazi party. I know that Nazi membership was not automatically conferred on men and women; it had to be applied for. I believe that most, if not all proprietors of businesses in Worpswede, became party members. However, even today I ask myself if, beyond a personal expression of solidarity with the Nazi regime, was party membership required or was it, in some cases, nothing but a formality? Did party membership assure protection from harassment by Party officials or prevent the closing of a business? I know that the merchants were highly visible in the community. Standing behind the counters and desks in their stores and offices they could not hide from the local Nazi officials. I am certain that they did not have the same opportunities as Worpswede's artists, for they could not seclude themselves at a writer's desk or hide behind the painter's easel. Therefore, can one accuse someone like Vater Reiners because of the party button on his lapel? I don't believe that further research can answer these questions for me, because the generation of Vater Reiners and his contemporaries is gone and I doubt that they left a written record concerning political commitment or survival.

What about Albert? Was his a youthful decision to join an organization that promised to confer power upon young men by wearing its uniform? Did he at one time believe in the tenets of National Socialism? I don't know, but he may have. Although at a young age I had separated my world into Nazis and anti-Nazis, into foes or friends, I now realize that I did not always adhere to the strict dividing line I had created for myself. There were people I liked very much and, because of that, I tried to reason that they could not have been "real" Nazis. The resulting inner conflict has not been resolved.

I did not extend this kind of tolerance to most of my teachers. I assumed, and in some cases I knew, that many of our teachers were Nazis but, to be honest, I did not like all of my teachers and it was easy to label them. Throughout my school years my nearly automatic assessment of who was a Nazi or an anti-Nazi created adversarial situations for me that did not promote learning. I probably did not consider political persuasion in the first and second grade; I only remember being eager to learn to read and write. However, by the time I entered third grade, which was taught by a Mr. Petersen, a person known to be a rabid supporter of Hitler and National Socialism, his political stance definitely influenced me. Mr. Peterson was a very strict teacher not only strict, but harsh. A week after I had skipped from third to fourth grade—also taught by Mr. Peterson in a combined classroom—I literally felt the sting of his harsh methods. Not knowing the answer to an unfamiliar arithmetic procedure, I was called to the front of the class, told to stretch out my hands and was twice struck across my palms with a bamboo stick. It was painful and demeaning. I also knew it was unjust. Was Mr. Peterson angry that I had skipped a grade and did he want to teach me a lesson in humility? Did he vent his anger against the artist population that was assumed to be anti-Nazi by picking on a child of that community? Mr. Peterson, at the time no more than in his early forties, died a year or two later. At his request he was buried in full uniform wrapped in the swastika flag. Although it was an unheard of request, even among Hitler supporters, his wish was granted.

By the time I entered the fifth grade in our small private school, a school that had a total of twenty-seven students over five grades, I had developed a very negative and disrespectful attitude toward most teachers even though I could not possibly know if all of them were Nazis. In retrospect, it seems to me that my stance of inner resistance to Nazi authority automatically extended toward all authority. I was not the only student to react in this way. Most of the students made it difficult for our teachers and they made it difficult for us. We received poor grades because of our behavior and we had no recourse. I don't remember worrying about it.

In the context of defying authority, one particular memory stands out. It was in the spring of 1942, nearly a year after the invasion of Russia, when a group of Russian prisoners-of-war were assigned to the village. Some of the prisoners worked on re-building a major road into Worpswede. The sand for the roadwork was transported to the site from a large sand pit on a narrow-gauge railway that ran just below our school grounds. Although our teachers had informed us that it was strictly forbidden to speak with prisoners-of-war—this being considered as "giving aid and comfort to the enemy"—it didn't take long for us to try to make some contact with the men. During recess, when our teachers turned their backs to us in their routine of walking up and down the schoolyard, some of us would walk close to the embankment and cautiously wave and smile at the prisoners. Then, guessing that they must be hungrier than we were, one of us would run down the embankment to give them parts of our sandwiches or an apple. Over a few weeks we gained smiles and we learned a few words of Russian—*dobre dien* (good day) and *spaciba* (thank you) stick in my mind. We felt happy and courageous.

In early September of 1942, due to the frequency of air raids, many of Bremen's schools, among them the girls' high school in which I had just enrolled, were evacuated to small towns in Upper Bavaria, an area in Southern Germany untouched by bombing. This program, under the auspices of the Nazi regime, was called *Kinderlandverschickung* (roughly translated as a program of "sending children into the countryside"); it was a program originally instituted in September of 1940 for the purpose of removing city children from the danger of air raids. In recent research I came across an article that stated that the evacuation was also instituted for the purpose of removing children from their parents in order to expose them to the daily influence of Nazi ideology. The writer of the article remembered that the evacuation program was at times cynically described as *Kinderlandverschleppung* (deportation of children into the countryside). However, our class was lucky, because the two teachers who accompanied us, Fräulein Cabisius and Fräulein Mahlstedt, were not Nazis and did not insist on daily political lectures or on political expressions (I don't remember any Heil Hitlers in our boarding house). Each day we followed a schedule of breakfast, morning classes, dinner, a rest period, afternoon homework session, outdoor sports, supper, and more homework or free time. We had to take care of our rooms and help the nuns in the kitchen—a favorite assignment, because the helper would get a little extra food to eat. On many afternoons we hiked in the foothills and mountains of the beautiful Alpine environment. Remarkably, our class of twenty students, ages fourteen and fifteen, along with two upper class students and our two teachers, lived quite harmoniously during our school year away from home. Yes, we were homesick at times, especially at Christmas, but we felt safe and cared for.

By the time our class returned to the high school in Bremen in early June of 1943, the number and intensity of air raids, both day and night, had further increased, and we spent more time in the basement of our school than in our classroom. A second school evacuation was arranged, but this time I did not participate because it became clear that the supervision of the second evacuation was to be firmly under Nazi leadership. According to my memory evacuation was not compulsory at the time; however, you had to prove that you were enrolled in another school. I was fortunate to be able to live with the family of my girlfriend Barbara, who lived close to Verden, a small town about sixty miles south-west of Worpswede where both of us enrolled in the local girls' high school. At that time Verden was considered a safe town—it experienced few if any air raids. However, we had not counted on the fact that the headmaster of the school was a stern and convinced Nazi. There was nothing but "Heil Hitler" here and "Heil Hitler" there throughout the whole school day. It was the most depressing school I can remember.

Perhaps it was the rigid and oppressive atmosphere that challenged me into open conflict with our art teacher. On the day she posted a copy of a painting on the wall, a pastoral scene painted in a *Sturm und Drang* style, of a tall, blond ploughman with muscular arms, guiding a pair of powerful horses along finely delineated furrows of dark, rich soil—I expressed what I thought of the unimaginative painting. I declared: "This is not art." The teacher raised her eyebrows and explained that this was the sort of art the *Führer* supported. I wasn't deterred by her statement and, bolstered by my pride of having grown up among artists, continued with my comments asserting that my mother's black and white photographs were more creative than the painting on the wall. The end result of this interchange was that I was to bring a sketch of my own to the next class, an example of the art I appreciated.

A week later I handed in my sketch, depicting a stand of poplars near a pond, drawn with a few strokes, hinting at leaves and leaving much room for imagination. No, it wasn't art, but it was in complete contrast to the painting on the wall, and that's the point I wanted to make. Nothing came of my open disagreement with the teacher, although a week later she returned the sketch with the comment that all teachers in the school had judged it to be without any artistic merit. I didn't care about their judgment. What was important to me was that I had stood my ground—the days of worrying about sweeping properly were behind me.

What did war feel like? In terms of schooling, I know that the war gave me a feeling of the meaninglessness of the learning process. Especially after a night of heavy bombing over Bremen (many of the students came from Bremen), when our class in the Verden girls' school would be informed in a manner alike to a news broadcast, that one of our classmates had been killed during the air raid. In keeping with the edict of silencing bad news, we were never given an opportunity to talk about or mourn her death. While we were left with feelings of guilt and sorrow, we also learned to accept death too easily. I know that I was angry and shocked at the immediacy of death, the violence of war, and the oppressive political atmosphere within the school, yet my classmates and I seemed to adapt to the conditions in silence. We were locked into a routine of uncertainty and fatigue due to having to rush into cellars during nighttime air raids, of facing hunger and cold, and numberless fears. I am now aware that our teachers lived under the same conditions.

Reflecting on World War II, I realize that air raids, more than any other aspect of the war, left the deepest impression on me. While I attended school in Worpswede, until mid-summer of 1942, I was not overly conscious of them. Nonetheless, because of our village's proximity to Bremen, sirens would blare in our village at least twice a week during the night, later on almost nightly, making us jump out of our beds and rush into our basement. We could hear the bombers as they circled overhead in their repeated approaches to their destination, the industrial city of Bremen. Only three times during the war bombs were dropped on our village. It was our understanding that the bombs were dropped because the British or American planes were damaged and needed to rid the plane of the weight of the bombs to assure a safe return to England. The first bomb was dropped in a large rye field—it left a huge crater, but didn't damage anything but the crops. The second bomb was dropped just outside of Worpswede, creating a crater in an open field. However, on that day not was only a bomb dropped, but the plane, a British bomber, crashed a short time later not far from the crater. The three-men crew was killed and shortly thereafter buried. I don't remember much about the crash, but I remember hearing that our minister, Pastor Bobzien, despite Nazi opposition, had insisted on giving the airmen a final resting place in Worpswede's cemetery. The final compromise with Nazi authorities was that their graves had to be a certain distance from the local graves. Some of us, perhaps most of the villagers, singly and furtively, visited the plain graves over the following weeks and months. Several times flowers were found on the graves. Who were these airmen? Did we have to consider them enemies or were they ordinary people, caught in a war they had not chosen? What about the families who had lost a son or a husband? Silent speculation and unanswered questions surrounded this event. After the war the remains of the airmen were returned to England.

The third bomb was dropped among the rye fields during a daytime air raid in the summer of 1944. The raid must have come without warning, because the sirens didn't blare and we didn't rush into our basement. My mother and my sister Angela were in the garden; I was upstairs resting on a couch, because I had a cold. Suddenly a powerful whistling coming from the direction of the sky could be heard. I had never heard a sound like it, but immediately knew it had to be a bomb. I rolled towards the outside wall—those were the safety instructions—wondering if the house would be hit and whether I would survive. The whistling stopped with a loud explosion. I opened my eyes—I was still upstairs on the couch. The house was still standing. I raced downstairs to look for Mami and Angela and found them safe and sound in the laundry kitchen where they had sought refuge when they heard the whistling. We were relieved to find each other unhurt, but we were shaken up. The garden was littered with small bomb splinters. My mother and sister were lucky to have escaped injury.

Were we afraid of air raids? Yes, I know that all of us were afraid on some level, yet age and the personality of our family members also played a role. I am sure that Mami, whose father and brother lived in Bremen, was most aware of the devastation and death that even one bomb could cause. She must have been concerned for all of us, but she was outwardly calm and didn't let fear rule our lives. My oldest sister, Charly, fearless and angry about the war and everything connected with it, wanted nothing but to be able to sleep through the night. If it had been up to her she would have never raced to the basement. My middle sister, Angela, was by nature more fearful and I remember the worried expression on her face as we sat silently, sleepily, in our basement. Being the youngest and most carefree, I believe that I assumed that nothing could happen to us.

After I transferred to the girls' high school in Bremen I became more conscious of the frequency of air raids and the devastation caused by bombing, because I was now in the target zone. I knew that the mantle of security that had existed for me in the village, could not shield me in Bremen or, later on, in Verden. On my weekly train rides from Verden, via Bremen to Worpswede, beginning in the fall of 1943 and lasting until spring of 1945, I observed the ever-increasing destruction of houses and factories in and around Bremen. It didn't seem possible that people could continue to live in the rubble; it didn't seem possible that people still had the energy and will to work in the damaged offices and factories.

As I retrieve the memory of the visible destruction of homes and factories I realize that I began to share the population's apparent acceptance of the outrage. Although I am aware that our emotional and physical energy was spent on personal survival that seemed to leave little room for worrying about the events that had overtaken our lives I am struck by the realization that we adapted to the conditions surrounding our lives without outward protest. Why was there no outcry about the horror of lives lost, about hunger and pain, about the intolerable living and working conditions? Was it fear of being branded a traitor and being deported to a concentration camp or was it a general dulling of emotions that generated this non-reaction? Was disassociation from the surrounding terror the only method that helped people cope? As we have gained in distance from World War II more authors have been willing to address these and similar probing questions. Yet can questions and sought-for explanations, can exploration of individual or universal responsibility or honest acknowledgment of human failure ever atone for the devastation of human life?

In the last year of World War II there were times when I believed and hoped that the increasing intensity of air raids would hasten the end of the war and therefore had to be accepted. I also believed that Germany deserved this punishment not only because of the terror Hitler had unleashed throughout Europe but additionally because of the apparently unquestioned support of the Nazi regime by the German people. At the same time I knew that there were opponents of Hitler and fascism, even though they were few in numbers and obviously ineffective. I remember the attempt on Hitler's life, which, for one brief moment, signaled the possibility of an end to the madness in and around us. However, the ever-present power of the regime, real and inferred, rendered the opposition helpless and hopeless. The war ran on and on. The horror was unceasing.

World War II finally drew to close in late April of 1945, although the last few weeks of the war seemed interminably long. After the high school in Verden closed in mid-March I returned home. Except for elementary schools in small communities, the educational system throughout northern Germany ground to a halt during the spring of 1945. With the advancing troops from East, South, and West (Russian, English, French, and American) Germany's transportation system came to a standstill and those who could hastened home before all rail service ceased. By now Haus Seekamp not only housed the three original families, but three additional families. Refugees from eastern Germany, fleeing the advancing Russian troops, had joined our households during the fall of 1944. Somehow all of us managed to exist together, sharing living space, one kitchen, and one bathroom, yet feeling the strain of unwanted closeness. The weather in March was cold and raw; the house was barely heated; everything around us was bleak.

One of the strangest and most unsettling sights arrived in Worps-wede during the dreary spring of 1945. I was standing by the window of my mother's office when a long column of silent men, apparently prisoners-of-war, slowly trudged into view. The men, dressed in rem-nants of uniforms, slowly walked up one of Worpswede's main streets, called *Adolf Hitler Straße*. They were headed in the direction of the sports stadium—originally a sand pit—a large circular area, open at one end, surrounded by high, weed-overgrown embankments. German soldiers, looking much like prisoners themselves, silently accompanied the prisoners. I remember seeing several of the men being half-carried by their comrades, their arms linked in support of each other; they looked as though they were ill or injured. It was a sorrowful sight—a march of the dead. No doubt the marchers were part of Germany's un-acknowledged retreat—human beings dragged through town after town, looking for safety. We didn't dare leave the house—out of shame and out of fear. We didn't even have any food to share with them, because the past winter had been worse than any other.

The march of the prisoners made a deep impression on most residents of Worpswede and it finally lifted the silence among some of them. The weary and disheveled appearance of the prisoners and their guards was like a bad omen of what was to come. Perhaps people could envision themselves as prisoners, walking from place to place, as the armies of Russia, France, England, and America were coming closer. Although an early curfew kept most residents at home in the evening, some people must have sneaked to the sports arena that night. On the following day, after the prisoners and their guards had left the village, talk was heard about the prisoners who had been huddling around small fires in distinctly separate areas of the large arena. People speculated why the prisoners kept a certain distance from each other. Someone seemed to know that the prisoners were Russians and Poles. Would the language barrier have kept them apart?

But weren't the languages quite similar? Perhaps they didn't trust each other? Didn't that prove that foreigners were untrustworthy? Everything about the prisoners was discussed, cautiously, always with an eye toward block wardens, although by now some people felt emboldened to speak in public spaces. The day had come when it was evident to many of the residents, except the staunchest Nazis, that the war was lost. We didn't see any more prisoners, but the event continued to be on our minds.

Within a matter of days another troop of soldiers, German soldiers, arrived and stayed in the village for a few days. The large downstairs gallery in Haus Seekamp was requisitioned for the officers. Other soldiers were housed in private homes throughout the village. Why did they pass through Worpswede? Perhaps they were regrouping, trying to figure out where they should go next? Despite the uncertainty of their future the soldiers seemed quite at ease; they had little or nothing to do, except to chat with people in the community. I remember the day when a few of them accompanied my sister Angela and me as we pulled a large wooden wagon, carrying an axe and a large saw, to the woods on the outskirts of Worpswede. We were getting firewood. Coal distribution was a thing of the past. I think the soldiers were surprised that two teenage girls were not afraid to chop down trees. I don't believe they had any idea how the civilian population existed during the war. They did not lend a hand.

The last week of April found the residents of Haus Seekamp huddling in the basement. The shelling of Worpswede had begun without any warning. Not even the sirens had blared the alert when the first rounds of artillery exploded in the village. We were eleven people in a basement that surely was not meant for living quarters. Until the beginning of the war it was meant to house two coal furnaces, coal bins, storage areas for canned goods, and an assortment of garden tools. Then, with the onset of the air war, chairs had been brought into the basement; likewise, room for suitcases and a shelf for foodstuffs had also been created. However, this time we didn't sit in the basement for a few hours; this time the basement became our living quarters for more than five days. I don't know how we spent our days, I don't remember how we slept at night, but somehow we managed to live in the basement, listening to the shelling and wondering if it would hit Haus Seekamp. It wasn't long before we realized that the artillery shelling was intermittent; this gave us time, usually twenty minutes, to run upstairs, cook some food, wash up, brush our teeth and go to the bathroom. Luckily, our electricity and our water were never cut off. Sometime during the fifth night, we heard voices upstairs, calling our names. It was our sister Charly. She and two girlfriends, had left the air force auxiliary unit to which they had been attached for nearly a year. They had gone AWOL and hitched rides on trains or walked the many miles from the north coast to get home to Worpswede before the war ended. We were surprised and overjoyed. Only Charly would have had the courage for such an undertaking.

The following day was the first day of May, a holiday in Germany—similar to Labor Day in the United States. For more than two hours we hadn't heard any shelling. My sisters and I decided to venture outside. We walked cautiously and slowly to the farthest corner of the garden from where we could see an intersection where three streets converged. It was a brilliant day, sunny and warm, and it was eerily quiet. When we approached our lookout spot we saw the first group of foreign soldiers, walking in a crouch and holding their rifles ready to shoot, at the intersection. What an amazing sight! The presence of foreign soldiers and no more firing into the village could only mean that the war was over for us. We raced back to the house, ran down the cellar steps, shouted our good news, asking everyone to come outdoors with us, into the sunshine and find out for themselves that Worpswede had been liberated. I don't know whether the refugees in our apartment had been Nazis or not, but it didn't matter any longer, because now we could say whatever we wanted to. What a remarkable moment! What a remarkable day!

Before long a few soldiers—British soldiers—came to the house and asked for the names of the residents as well as other information. Finally the English we had learned in school came in handy. Even Frau Seekamp, who had once visited friends in the United States, was able to communicate with the British. The rest of the day went by in a blur. In the early evening we gathered downstairs in Frau Seekamp's living room where the residents of Haus Seekamp, along with a number of British soldiers, drank a toast to the end of the war. Earlier that afternoon Mami had sent my sisters and me into the garden to dig up the few bottles of wine that we had buried a few weeks earlier in the gooseberry bushes. Why had she insisted that we bury the wine? She told us that she had been afraid that the end of the war would bring soldiers into the area who might get intoxicated and plunder.

We were relieved and happy as we toasted each other and sang English songs. I remembered one well-known English ballad from my English class in Verden "Drink to me only with thine eyes and I will drink with mine." When our teacher had taught us this song, he had commented that he wasn't certain that it was a proper song for young ladies of sixteen and seventeen and I now wondered what he would have said if he could see our family and friends toasting and singing with the British. The war was over! Not only was the war over, Nazism was over! It was an indescribable feeling! We could talk about anything we wanted to; no one could report on us. Ever since I could remember we had lived under the control of the Nazi regime, having to watch every word uttered in public—not anymore! Although the war did not officially end until the eighth of May, for us the war was over. Gone from one minute to the next!

Yet it didn't take long for us to realize that the consequences of war were not over for anyone, for now we were confronted with the enormity of the Nazi crimes. As the news of what had happened in the concentration camps became public we were sickened and horrified. Despite the fragments of information we had received from various sources during the war, nothing could have prepared us for the dimension of brutality and death in the concentration camps. The horror went deep; the shame went deep. The joy and the beauty of the first day of May disappeared with the news of German atrocities. Could anyone ever atone for this inhumanity?

Day-to-day life and its many demands returned and submerged, at least for a few hours each day, the oppressive news. Haus Seekamp was requisitioned as officers' quarters for the American detachment, which occupied Worpswede from June 1945 until early 1946. Within a matter of hours, my family as well as the other families had to leave our apartments, with only our clothes, some books and writing materials, as well as pots and dishes. The nearby church's fellowship hall, originally a large barn, was made available to some of us. Frau Seekamp, Ellida and her two children, along with her friend and her son, my mother, my two sisters and I, lived in the communal hall for several days. We slept on bunk beds, outfitted with straw mattresses. We cooked on an outdoor fire—luckily there were no rainy days. However, within a week or more all of us found apartments of our own and our little community of residents of Haus Seekamp had to separate after sharing our lives and trusting each other during the fateful years of World War II.

I now know why Mami could not answer my question on the last Sunday in August of 1939. I believe that, more than wanting to shield us from her memories of World War I, from the pain of hunger and insecurity of those years, she feared that nothing could prepare us for this war, a war which had begun with Hitler's rise to power in 1933. The crusade against Jewish people, against Socialists and Communists, against anyone who did not commit to the Nazi tenets, had been in force for years. Then, with the start of World War II, persecution, an integral part of Hitler's method of governing, was paired with the missionary zeal of global conquest in the name of *Lebensraum* and to fulfill his dream of a thousand year Third Reich. Even though Mami could not have foreseen the horror of what was to come, she seemed aware of the power and ruthlessness of the Nazi dictatorship. I try to imagine her thoughts and feelings as she faced the responsibility of protecting her three children from the harm of war and fascism.

If my children and grandchildren should now ask me: "What does war feel like?" I will try to tell them that war is more than a feeling. I will speak to them of my perceptions that war is reality and unreality, a time when ethics and reasoning are converted into a self-serving rationale for military conquest, a time when killing and devastation are glorified as expressions of courage and national pride. I will share my understanding that the consequences of all wars are the destruction of lives of both "winners" and "losers," for no one can escape its injustice, its immorality, cruelty, and horror. I will tell my children and grandchildren that I perceive World War II as unique among wars as it incorporated not only a government's greed for land and power, but was based on Hitler's deep-seated and limitless hatred of Jewish people, a hatred with which he contaminated nearly a whole nation. I will explain to them that Hitler's obsession with "cleansing" Germany of the stranger, the person not "Germanic," became the reason for the extermination of millions of Jews. Yet, while trying to answer their questions, I have to qualify my answers and acknowledge that my observations, far from ghettos and concentration camps, far from the "killing fields" and bombed-out cities, are mere gleanings of childhood impressions. I need to admit to them that my search for answers continues, just as my questions never cease.

HAUS IM SCHLUH

Profile of Betsi Hecker by Birgit Nachtwey

"Today the painter Margarete Hecker, known as Bezi among friends and family, is almost unknown among the residents and artists of Worpswede. She was born in Berlin in 1913 and attended school in Hannover, where her family had moved shortly after her birth. Pursuing her love and enthusiasm of acting Bezi enrolled in an actor's school in Berlin in the early thirties. However, after only a short time, she left her acting studies and dedicated herself to painting and drawing while attending an art academy in Hannover. She continued her art studies in Munich, where her young talent was soon recognized. In 1934, on a bicycle tour through Schleswig-Holstein (northern Germany), Bezi, on her return trip to Hannover, stopped in Worpswede and, while there, discovered the artists' refuge of Haus im Schluh. Worpswede and Haus im Schluh appeared to her the perfect place where she could develop her painting, a community seemingly untouched by the oppressive effects of Nationalist-Socialist power politics.

"Although Bezi continued her connections with Hannover where a number of assignments were still awaiting completion, she chose Worpswede as her home in that same year. Haus im Schluh and the

Schluh family of creative women and men became her first homestead in the artist colony. This is where she received the support and encouragement to continue and develop her painting. Ellida von Alten, a painter and writer and a friend of the Schluh community, became her trusted friend. Soon Bezi was able to find an apartment and studio on the property of the well-known farmer Nikolaus Böttjer, who was a major supporter of Worpswede's artists.

"In 1940, during a show of Margarete Hecker's paintings in Hannover, the work of the young artist was declared "degenerate" by the officialdom of the Nazi regime and her paintings were removed from the gallery. It was a severe shock to her; the first of several devastating events to follow. Soon thereafter many of her paintings were destroyed during an air raid on Hannover, and, in 1944, personal tragedy followed. In order to circumvent being drafted into the German Nurses Corps and accept an assignment to a military hospital in the East (probably Russia), Bezi was persuaded to undergo an operation to remove her appendix, an operation not considered essential although prescribed by her physician as necessary. She left Worpswede and moved to the home of relatives in Bavaria and underwent the operation from which she did not recover. Depressed about the many unfinished paintings, paintings not even conceived, she died, a promising and talented artist, missed greatly by her friends in the Schluh community.

"The paintings Margarete Hecker left are primarily portraits and still-lives, a few landscapes, as well as many watercolors of the Worpswede landscape. Some of the paintings were stolen by the American Occupation Forces in 1945 and no one knows where they are now. Others are still owned by friends and family, tucked away from public view. Those circumstances, and the fact that her paintings had not been exhibited since 1940, have contributed to Margarete Hecker being forgotten for many years. However, rediscovered through the few paintings recently traced, Margarete

Hecker is re-emerging as an artist whose work deserves much more attention than has been paid to her until now."

The above, a translation of Birgit Nachtvey's article by Christa Meiners-DeTroy, was published by Worpsweder Verlag in 1995 in the book Station Schluh *memorializing seventy-five years of the art community Haus im Schluh (pages 26-28).*

*My own, scant memories of Bezi Hecker
during the years 1942–1944.*

In January 1942, when I was thirteen and a half years old, the artist Bezi Hecker asked me to sit for her—something that was not unusual in the artist colony, where painters were always looking for models. Bezi offered me fifty cents for each sitting and a little snack besides. Not only was this an offer I could not refuse, but Bezi was also a close friend of our family and I was pleased that she wanted to paint a portrait of me.

The first time I went to sit for Bezi she surprised me by asking me to take my glasses off. I had begun to wear glasses only a few years earlier and had been relieved when I was finally able to see a teacher's writing on the blackboard, see individual leaves on trees and recognize my friends from a distance. Bezi, not wearing glasses, explained to me that she herself was very nearsighted, but she didn't consider it a handicap. Not only that, but according to her, nature and people, being less clearly defined, looked softer and more beautiful to her when she did not wear glasses. She also assured me that my sight would not improve by wearing glasses, so why wear them all the time? Despite my mother's dismay I was persuaded by Bezi's argument and followed her suggestion immediately.

Portrait of Christa Meiners-DeTroy.
Painting by Betsi Hecker, 1942

I enjoyed sitting for Bezi. There wasn't much conversation during the painting sessions. Bezi painted with great concentration and I had to sit very still, but I felt comfortable in her presence. I vividly remember the plate of fruit in front of me, in particular the orange. Since it was wartime we seldom, if ever, saw oranges in our village grocery store—I believe Bezi must have bought the fruit in the city. Naturally, the fruit could not be eaten, because she needed it for her painting and it would be nearly impossible to replace it. At first it was an ordeal to have the tempting fruit in front of me.

As promised Bezi gave me a treat before I went home. During the cold and snowy winter months she concocted a delicious mixture of cottage cheese and strawberry preserve. Not having a refrigerator (perhaps half a dozen homes in Worpwede had refrigerators in those days) she would place a pan with the mixture into a small mound of snow in her front yard. I don't know how long it was left in the snow, but by the time we took the tray out of its hiding place the concoction was nearly frozen. For a child starved for sweets, this was worth much more than the fifty cents I received for each sitting. I know that our grocery store did not carry strawberry preserves during the war, but I believe that Bezi's mother sent her such treats off and on—they had a large farm and garden and raised fruits and vegetables. After moving to the U.S. in 1947, I attempted to duplicate the cottage cheese recipe, but it never tasted the same. Regretfully I have had to accept that Bezi's treat, along with other experiences, belongs to a past as something that cannot be recreated.

Bezi made a deep impression upon me for a number of reasons. Not only was Bezi a tall and striking young woman, a quiet person, friendly and thoughtful, but she was also a serious woman, surrounded by an aura of isolation and remoteness. I admired Bezi's work and dedication to her art. Most of all I felt comfortable with Bezi, because she, like so many of the Worpswede artists, treated children with respect. Without words I sensed that she had an innate appreciation of all human beings and that age differences between adults and children did not present a barrier to acceptance and friendship.

My next memory of Bezi is associated with a vacation during the summer of 1942. My mother, my sister Angela, and I spent our summer vacation in a small Alpine village in Upper Bavaria, close to the farm Bezi's family had bought as a summer refuge from the city of Hannover. I loved being on the farm, loved the big Hecker family of five daughters (Bezi was the oldest) and one son, Peter, who was my age. We hiked, went mountain climbing, went swimming, and helped with the haying—it was a wonderful vacation. Yet the dark shadow of Nazism intruded even into this summer's interlude. While Betsi's mother and siblings were fervently anti-Nazi, Betsi's father (away from the farm at that time) was a supporter of the Nazi regime. Peter, who shared his mother's views until that summer decided near the end of our vacation he would align himself with his father and became an active member of the boys' division of the Hitler Youth. He, who had become a good friend of mine, became utterly obnoxious during the last few days of our vacation and we parted with hostile words—sneers (his) and tears (mine). I remember my furious bicycle ride back to our vacation cottage and ending up in my mother's arms, sobbing. Strong feelings about politics had broken up our friendship. However, in retrospect, I realize that it was also the inevitable end of a summer friendship.

My mother and sister returned to Worpswede and a few weeks later Bezi also returned to her little house and studio at Nikolaus Böttcher's farm close to our home. Later that summer, in early September, I returned to Bavaria, to the town of Bad Wiessee, as part of a school program (*Kinderlandverschickung*) that evacuated school children from large cities to rural areas, in order to protect them from air raids. The evacuation took place shortly after my mother had enrolled me in a high school in Bremen.

I didn't see Bezi again until July of 1943—a few weeks after I had returned from Bad Wiessee. My memories of that summer are vague. The daily routine of helping at home, working in the garden, cycling to the river for a swim and spending time with family and friends may not have seemed important enough to consign it to memory. However, the nightly air raids over the nearby city of Bremen, rushing into the basement when the sirens screamed their warning, the sound of the airplanes circling above Worpswede, the obituaries of young soldiers, ration cards, and the constant awareness of the Nazi presence, continue to stand out.

My last clear memories of Bezi are of my summer vacation in 1944—the six weeks when I was home from school and enjoyed our close community of family and friends on a daily basis. On many of that summer's warm afternoons Bezi would join our family, her close friend Ellida von Alten and her children for conversation and a glass of juice in the common garden of the Haus Seekamp residents. I think it was in late June that my mother mentioned that Bezi would be going south for a few weeks. Since Bezi visited her family in Bavaria on a regular basis, her leaving did not make a specific impression on me, especially so since no one had spoken of an unusual reason for her leaving. Thus it was a disturbing discovery, when, only recently, I read the profile of Bezi in the book *Station Schluh* (cited above) and became aware of the significance of her trip to Bavaria. However, at the time Bezi's trip south did not seem extraordinary. I only remember wishing that I could go with her in order to spend another vacation in the Alps. A couple of weeks after Bezi left Angela and I heard from our mother and Ellida that Bezi was ill and had to have an operation. Neither of them expressed serious worries about her medical condition at that time.

To this day I visualize my sister Angela and I standing under the pear tree in our garden as our mother and Ellida stood in silence on the garden path. After a few minutes they addressed us and told us with few words that Bezi had died. In response to my questions about Bezi's illness and death I heard my mother's mysterious comment: "Bezi had lost the will to live." What did that mean? A painful and uneasy silence hid the circumstances of her death from us. Sad and confused I didn't pressure the adults to tell us more—it didn't seem to be the time to bother the adults with my feelings and questions.

The information about the reason for Bezi's death, as written in the book *Station Schluh,* was a shocking revelation to me. Until I read her profile, I neither knew about the official designation of Bezi's paintings as "degenerate" nor about the subsequent removal of her paintings from the art gallery; I had never heard of the loss of many of her works of art during air raids on Hannover. In retrospect I perceive a connection between the sentence "Depressed about the unfinished paintings, paintings not even conceived" (*Station Schluh*, p. 26) and my mother's statement: "Bezi had lost the will to live." As I contemplate my memories and reflect on the recent article about her I think that a kind of hopelessness must have invaded Bezi's life after the Nazis sought her out—first in Hannover and then in Worpswede, a place she had considered a safe haven for herself and her art. She must have been devastated and angry that her art was branded "degenerate" and thus removed from public view; she must have felt helpless and despondent when the Nazi authorities decided that she could no longer be a painter, but should be sent to the Eastern front as a nurse. She must have felt that her vision and identity as an artist were deliberately and systematically erased. I often think of Bezi and wonder why this beautiful and gifted artist had to die at the age of thirty-one—another victim of the Nazi regime.

Although I have few memories of Bezi she continues to be on my mind not only because of the winter of 1942 when she painted my portrait and shared her presence and the delicious dessert with me but because of the quiet kindness and thoughtful acceptance she offered me and her many friends throughout her few years in Worpswede. What was then an indistinct awareness of the presence of the sorrow that shadowed her brief life has now been confirmed through the recent information.

Rolled up in her suitcase, my mother brought Bezi's portrait of me to the United States in the mid-1970s. Put on a stretcher, but unframed, the painting hung in our home for nearly thirty years. A few years ago, it became obvious that it needed to be restored—the oil paints and the canvas available to Bezi during the war years had been of poor quality and the paint began to fade and flake off. Early this year, urged on by writing about my childhood memories,

I decided to go ahead with the restoration of the portrait. Beautifully reconditioned and newly framed, the painting now hangs in my living room in Brunswick, Maine. It is a constant reminder of Bezi, of her creativity and serious dedication to her art, as well as the wonderful connections and experiences we shared in Worpswede and during the summer in the Alps. Other memories also come to the fore, the oppression of the Nazi regime, the war, the separations, the fear and powerlessness that over-shadowed all our lives—that took Bezi's life.

Heavy frost on a birch -- January 1941. Photo by JMB

KINDERLANDVERSCHICKUNG

"School Evacuation during World War II"

In late July or early August of 1942, close to two months before I turned fourteen, the small private middle school (fifth through ninth grade) in Worpswede, closed its doors. I don't know the details of the origin of the *Mittelschule*, how many years the school had been in operation or the exact reasons for its closing. However, I can assume that running the school was no longer financially tenable, because the entire student body, distributed over five grades, seldom numbered more than thirty girls and boys. Throughout the nearly four years I attended the school my own class was made up of only three students—Waldtraut, Hans, and me. When the school shut its doors most of its students elected to transfer to the nearest middle school, a six-year co-ed high school in Osterholz-Scharmbeck, a railroad center and county seat about ten miles southwest of Worpswede. The remainder of the students, including me, transferred to various *Oberschulen* (eight-year girls' or boys' high schools) in the city of Bremen. For some reason my mother decided that I should attend the girls' high school *Oberschule für Mädchen an der Karlstraße* [High School for Girls on Karl Street] in Bremen, a decision I wasn't happy with, because all of my girlfriends went to the school in Osterholz-Scharmbeck. From one week to the next my whole world changed.

Gone were the days when I could get up after seven o'clock in the morning and walk or run the short distance to school. Gone were the days of walking home to a hot midday meal and spending afternoons at home or with my friends. Without any warning the familiarity of Worpswede school days and having close friends disappeared. From then on each school day began with a pre-dawn walk to the train station to catch the early *Arbeiterzug* [the factory workers' train] to Osterholz-Scharmbeck where I had to change trains for the trip to Bremen. Until then I had had few occasions to travel to the city by myself and I felt quite unsure about making the daily round-trip between Worpswede and Bremen that entailed catching the train on time, making the connection in Osterholz, and getting across Bremen's busy streets on my way to the new school. Then, once I arrived at Karlstrasse, I was confronted with a large class of girls (any number over five seemed large to me), who were complete strangers, a different and expanded curriculum, and new, more demanding, teachers. It turned out to be a difficult beginning. Only the fact that my mother seemed convinced that I was able to make the transition from our local school to the high school in Bremen helped me cope with the changes.

However, it turned out that this was not the only change that summer. A few weeks later, it may have been in late August or early September, students of the Karlstrasse and their parents were informed that Bremen's high school population was to be evacuated to small towns in Upper Bavaria, areas remote from the ever-increasing bombing raids. At the time I may have believed that only the Bremen schools were to be evacuated; however, I later learned that the government-sponsored evacuation affected high school students of many large cities throughout Germany. Although some of the schools

66

in Bremen continued to hold classes, parents were urged to participate in the evacuation program or to send their children to the relative safety of schools in towns well beyond the city limits of Bremen. My mother chose to enroll me in the evacuation program. I know that she was concerned about my daily train trips into Bremen, a city that was beginning to experience an increase in daytime bombing raids. As for my part in the decision-making, the fact that I had spent my previous summer vacation in Upper Bavaria and had come to love the mountains convinced me to participate in an adventure that would take me back to the Alps.

I remember the day of departure from Bremen's *Hauptbahnhof,* the imposing brick train station, with its domed, glassed-in roof, from which enumerable glass panes were missing—the result of nearby bomb explosions. Children and parents filled the platforms where a special passenger train, a *Sonderzug,* stood waiting for us. As I am writing this, more than sixty years after the event, I am chilled by the word *Sonderzug,* because I learned years later that this definition was commonly applied to trains that deported Jews, political prisoners and other "undesirables" to concentration camps. However, I was oblivious of this connection the day our class took the train to Upper Bavaria.

Reflecting on that day and visualizing the large crowds of girls and boys—students of Bremen's girls' high schools and boys' high schools were traveling on the same train—I wonder who made sure that students of the different high schools climbed into the right cars and compartments. Who saw to it that we were all accounted for? Much of what happened that day is now a blur, erased by time and the overriding emotions of excitement and apprehension I felt. However, I clearly remember the moment when the train was ready to pull out of the station. My classmates and I crowded around the open windows of adjoining compartments and looked out at family members—listening to last admonishments and bracing for the farewells. After the conductor's shrill whistling and a wave of his round red sign, the train moved slowly through the station. Parents and children waved and called out to family members: *Auf Wiedersehen! Auf Wiedersehen!* for as long as they were in sight. Many of us continued to stand at the windows for a while longer, looking at the disappearing city as the train left Bremen. In my mind's eye I can still see the front and rear train sections, which were simultaneously visible as we rounded a long curve. Since our families had passed from sight by then students spontaneously waved to one another as if to encourage each other on our way to an unfamiliar destination. Today I wonder if the children's train was a happy sight as it moved through the countryside or was there a touch of sadness as hundreds of children were removed from their families under the auspices of the Nazi government?

It is nearly impossible to retrieve the details of the trip as we traveled south through the afternoon and night. However, I remember the sense that our class was on its own throughout most of our journey to Upper Bavaria. Although I am sure that two of our teachers accompanied our class I don't recall seeing them during the trip; perhaps they sat in another section of the train? Two older students, who functioned in an assistant supervisory capacity, looked in on us from time to time to make sure that we ate our sandwiches for the evening meal. After that we settled in our seats for the night. No doubt it was my deep awareness that I faced a long separation from my family, accentuated by the fact that I still felt like a stranger among my classmates, that made me feel completely alone on that day.

Our train arrived at our destination, Bad Wiessee, a small, but well-known spa, situated on the shore of Lake Tegernsee, sometime during the following morning. It was just a short trip by bus from the train station to our new home, St. Josefsheim, a combination boarding house and bed-and-breakfast, run by Catholic nuns. The home was one of many facilities, large and small, requisitioned by the Nazi government to house students or convalescing soldiers during the war. I recall the day we arrived in Bad Wiessee as a radiant day. The warm sunshine, the vivid colors of flower boxes full of cascading geraniums in front of the homes, views of green meadows reaching toward forested mountain ranges and the friendly welcome by the nuns of St. Josefsheim are clear and happy memories. Everything seemed beautiful to me! My loneliness evaporated.

Once our class had settled into our new home, our teachers quickly put a daily schedule into place that it consisted of meals, classes, homework, afternoon naps as well as daily hikes into the foothills of the nearby mountains. Naturally, we also had to take care of our rooms and, on a rotating basis, help the nuns in the kitchen. Our teachers, Fräulein Cabisius (math and science) and Dr. Dening (German, English, geography and history), were exceptional people. They were thoughtful and friendly and didn't seem to be Nazis. How did I arrive at that conclusion? I believe I had a sixth sense about people and their politics; a display of genuine friendliness was a defining factor for me. The fact that our teachers didn't insist on our shouting Heil Hitler at each other throughout the day (actually, I don't recall ever having to say Heil Hitler to anyone in the home; but then again, I may have blocked that memory out) and did not push any kind of political agenda on us, confirmed my intuition. Yet I know that we weren't completely free of Nazi supervision. A young woman, responsible for the inclusion of certain political requirements in our daily schedule, augmented the teaching staff in St. Josefsheim. Her tasks included overseeing student attendance at evening news reports and conducting a weekly "political evening." (I had completely forgotten the presence of the political supervisor until I recently re-read a letter, dated April 11, 1943, from Fräulein Cabisius to my mother, in which she referred to the young woman. Evidently she did not leave much of an impression on me.) In a letter to my family, dated November 30, 1942, I describe one of the political evenings, telling my mother and sisters that most of my classmates wanted to go to bed early on those evenings because we didn't want to participate in the program. My concluding sentence, written later that evening, reads: *"Der politische Abend war höchst blöde—wir sind alle froh, daß er zuende ist"* (The political evening was very stupid and all of us are happy that it's over). Although I was generally cautious about making political comments in my letters home I must have felt that it would not have been unusual for fourteen-year olds to consider political discussions boring.

I am grateful that my mother saved a number of the letters I wrote to her and my sisters for they retrieved many of the experiences of the year in Bad Wiessee. Most of my letters deal with ordinary events, such as describing our daily routine, our various classes, upcoming tests, homework, hiking, and helping Sister Petrina, a favorite of all the students, in the kitchen. Thinking of Sister Petrina brings a flood of memories into the present. For one, I remember that I wasn't known for volunteering in the kitchen at home, but it was different at St. Josefsheim where the nuns praised me for being helpful and quick, whether drying dishes or preparing vegetables. I recall that I loved spending time in the kitchen, because it meant getting away from schedules and having to be quiet. The kitchen was a cheerful place and there was much laughter. Another positive aspect of kitchen duty was the occasional extra slice of bread or even a piece of cake given to us—something each student treasured. In my letters home I frequently refer to our meals, describing them as being very good, although not always as plentiful as we may have wished. 1942 was the third year of the war and diminishing food rations affected everyone. As active teenagers we were always hungry. I remember being thankful when, at mealtimes, it was my turn to take the last slice of bread, the heel, out of the basket, for it was the thickest slice and it provided more nourishment. To this day I'm partial to the heel of a loaf of bread.

Even though the focus of my letters home dealt primarily with daily life in St. Josefsheim, I touched on politics off and on. I was cautious about expressing political opinions, because of my fear that postal authorities might open my letters. However, if I made a political observation I used neutral expressions in describing one or another event and, in reference to my fellow students, I used words like "sensible" or "reasonable," indicating that they weren't raving Nazis. I don't believe that I discussed politics with any of my class-mates during the first couple of months in Bad Wiessee. It was not safe to trust anyone—even if one sensed that a classmate was not a Nazi.

When I reflect on our year in Bad Wiessee, I believe it must have been very difficult for most of us, far from our families and not being allowed to speak freely about the issues that were on our minds. As I recall, there was an extensive, although unwritten list of subjects we didn't dare speak about: no comments about air raids and hunger; no questions about the war and the safety of family members in Bremen or other towns. These concerns could not be discussed, because anything that appeared as worry or doubt could suggest that one did not trust the Hitler regime and this, in turn, could have political consequences.

Within this context I remember Fräulein Cabisius' announcement (I don't remember the month or the season) to our assembled class that our classmate Almuth's older sister, a university student in Munich, had accidentally died in that city. The veiled, terse statement by our teacher led me to believe that the real story could not be told. Why did I assume that her death appeared to have a connection to politics, perhaps to a student resistance movement? What made me think of that? I don't remember. (Through later reading and research I believe that her sister was part of the White Rose movement.) I do remember that I didn't dare ask Almuth any questions about her sister, because I was afraid to reveal my political views to her, even though I sensed she shared them. I try to recall how we consoled Almuth without touching on the cause on her sister's death. I know we treated her with carefully expressed kindnesses, while, at the same time, surrounding her and her grief with silence. We were so young and death at such close proximity was frightening. Almuth, who had always been more serious and remote than the rest of my classmates, was even more quiet and withdrawn after the death of her sister. A short time later she had an epileptic episode during Algebra class. Fräulein Cabisius assisted her immediately, while most of us stayed in our chairs, paralyzed by fear—we didn't know what to do. Once the episode had subsided and Almuth had been taken to her room, our teacher took the opportunity to explain epilepsy to us. However, knowledge could not remove my fear and discomfort. Today, as I am thinking of Almuth I realize that it was angst of the barely understood that caused our timid reaction to the mystery of unexpected death and illness surrounding her. Sadly, I recall that I chose the safety of silence instead of comforting words. Silence, although troubling, was my frequent refuge.

Another event that confused and troubled me for a long time relates to our class's required movie attendance in town. My letters home confirm that we saw films on a weekly basis and that we generally went in small groups to the local movie theater. However, one day, it must have been a Saturday in early spring, we were told that we had to march, dressed in Hitler Youth uniforms, to the theater. What was that all about? Some order from high up? We were told to go to a room in the basement of St. Josefsheim where we would find a large bureau with drawers full of uniforms in different sizes. We

Class photo taken during the school evacuation in Bad Wiessee. Christa is circled in white.(1942-43) Photo by JMB.

ran downstairs and tried on the navy blue skirts and white blouses, along with navy blue kerchiefs and small brown leather slipknots. Not everyone could find the right size and there was considerable pulling and tucking in while getting dressed. Before long all of us were all outfitted in uniforms and ready to march to the theater. It was an unsettling experience. Although I felt uncomfortable in the uniform I was also aware of a feeling of solidarity with the marching group. Was it the number of girls or was it the uniform that gave me this feeling? I remember the fleeting thought that no one could do anything to us as long as we wore the uniform, because it was unthinkable that anyone would say anything out loud against a person in a Hitler Youth uniform.

Despite the fact that we, as northern Germans, were not well liked in Bavaria (we were called "dirty Prussians" by local children when we walked into town), I had never felt threatened by any of the children. For that matter, some of us would retaliate by calling them "dirty Bavarians" and feel vindicated by our bravado. However, being in uniform and marching in a troop, gave me a different feeling: it wasn't a sense of safety, but a sense of being superior and invincible. Could wearing a uniform change me from one moment to the next? Was I suddenly part of the Nazi movement? Was I succumbing to group mentality, ready to give up my individuality? As I am writing this, more than sixty years later, I am able to examine my reaction in more detail and with deeper insight. I do remember the feeling of confusion and distress by my response to the uniform and marching. Did I share my thoughts and feelings with anyone? I don't think so. Thus, another discomforting experience was silenced, yet never erased. Recently I came across a letter to my mother, in which I describe part of the episode of that day: "On Saturday we saw the movie *Stukas* (for a second time!). This time it was a mandatory attendance and we were required to dress in uniforms. The skirts were too short, the blouses too short, but we had to wear them. The film was horrible and our whole class, except for a few, swore never to go to such a frightening film again. Most of us feel the same way about the weekly newsreels, because the photos are so cruel. Luckily, most of my classmates are sensible."

Beyond the silence, political evenings, uniforms, and violent movies, I have many good memories of our school year in Bad Wiessee. Our teachers, along with the nuns, provided a caring environment for us. They held birthday celebrations and arranged a beautiful Christmas for all of us; they encouraged music, singing, poetry readings, and supported our efforts to produce plays. We had a wonderful art teacher, who came for an afternoon of drawing once a week—one of my favorite activities. We enjoyed hiking on an almost daily basis; in the winter there was skiing and sledding; there were other sports according to the seasons. Except for one classmate, who could not bear to be away from her family and was sent home shortly after our arrival, there was little obvious homesickness. We were a cheerful group of girls, busy with school and developing friendships within our homogeneous group. However, it is likely that the primary reason for feeling comfortable in St. Josefsheim, was that we felt safe. Until I recently revisited my memories of the school year in Bad Wiessee, I had never connected the issue of safety with my heretofore-unacknowledged fear of the bombing in and around Bremen. As a child of war I lived with the assumption that I could manage to deal with and dodge the inner and outer exigencies of bombing and chaos. However, this assumption dissolved into thin air once I admitted to myself that the feeling of safety and well-being in Bad Wiessee had to be based on the absence of air raids. While most of my letters home cheerfully describe our daily activities, I repeatedly express my concern for my mother's and sisters' health and daily survival. Did they have enough to eat? Did they have enough coal to keep the furnace going? Did they experience many air raids during the night? With this in mind, I am certain that living in a safe environment created inner conflict for all of us, especially for those classmates whose families lived in the center of Bremen and were exposed to almost daily bombing. No doubt, our teachers created a full schedule of activities for us in order to counteract and soothe those conflicts—and it worked. Although it was natural for us to worry about our families, generally alone and in silence, being fully occupied didn't allow us to dwell on our feelings of helplessness.

Among my most significant memories of the year in Bad Wiessee, supported by my frequent letters home, was my developing friendship with Barbara. From the day I entered the girls' high school *Karlstrasse* in Bremen, she had easily stood out among my classmates as a kind and cheerful girl and I hoped that we would become friends. Living in the close community of St. Josefsheim gave all students a chance to become better acquainted and it wasn't long before Barbara and I developed a warm friendship. In early January our teachers decided to make some changes in room assignments and, much to our delight, Barbara and I were assigned a double room. After some tentative discussions we discovered that our families were firmly anti-Nazi, which deepened our bond. We were relieved that we had each other to turn to when we were troubled about the war and Nazi issues, when we had concerns about our families up north, about homework and daily life in St. Josefsheim. Now, sharing a room, we could hold conversations in complete privacy, something we treasured. During one of those private conversations we agreed to abstain from giving the required Hitler Youth oath during an upcoming ceremony. The occasion was our class's official promotion from *Jungmädel* to the next Hitler Youth level, the *Bund deutscher Mädel*, the organization for girls who had reached the age of fourteen. After a lengthy discussion, trying to figure out how we could circumvent the oath, Barbara and I devised the following plan: we would stand in the back row during the ceremony and only mouth the words of the oath—but never speak them. This, we agreed, would nullify our membership in the Hitler Youth, as well as sever any connection to National Socialism. I remember feeling courageous as we stood silently in the last row—and I know that we felt proud once the ceremony was over, even though our action remained hidden from everyone except us.

As Barbara and I became better acquainted I learned that she came from a religious household and, although we did not share a similar background, I was very interested in Christianity and fervently wished that her example as a believer would deepen my faith. Growing up within the artists' colony of Worpswede, where few of the artists were churchgoers, I hadn't given religion much thought. To be sure, the local Lutheran Church and our pastor occupied a place of honor and respect throughout the village; certainly, there were Christian traditions in which most of Worpswede's residents participated, as did my family. For instance, the holidays of Christmas, Easter and Pentecost were universally celebrated in church and at home. Other aspects of being part of a Christian community included the annual ceremony of confirmation of the village's sons and daughters, who, at age fourteen, became church members. I also recollect the familiar Sunday morning sight of parishioners, most of them farmers and their wives, slowly walking or bicycling to church in their black Sunday clothes. Another significant event connected to religion was the discomforting sight of the horse-drawn black-draped hearse followed by mourners on foot as they slowly wound their way up to the church on the hill for a funeral service. All of these church related traditions were part of my growing up. Yet, not until I was old enough to attend confirmation classes did religion and personal faith begin to enter my consciousness.

In the spring of 1941 I was enrolled in the first year of the two-year cycle of confirmation classes in Worpswede, a requirement that would lead to my confirmation in the spring of 1943. However, being evacuated to Upper Bavaria in September of 1942 meant that I would have to complete my religious studies in Bad Wiessee or wait another year in order to finish confirmation classes at home. Apparently my mother did not want to postpone my confirmation until 1944 and, with this in mind, she turned to our head teacher and asked if it could be arranged that I continue confirmation classes in order to be ready for confirmation while in Bad Wiessee, away from the customary celebration with family and neighbors. I never thought to ask my mother why she insisted on this.

There's one memory of a confirmation class in Worpswede that remains very vivid. I had known Worpswede's minister, Pastor Bobzien and his family for some time, because I used to play with their young children as an occasional "baby sitter." As an openhearted and friendly family they were easy to like. After attending church services and confirmation classes for some months I became acquainted with Pastor Bobzien as a minister and teacher. I grew to admire him for not being the typical "hell and damnation" kind of preacher often found in small villages. Most importantly, our pastor encouraged us to raise questions during the weekly classes. Until then, my relationship with teachers had not been based on the knowledge they were trained to teach, but on their authority within the classroom and, in particular, paired with the ever-present threat of Nazi authority and obedience to the State. Even though Pastor Bobzien was not a schoolteacher, I assumed he would use the same authoritarian approach. However, his classes were quite different. The pastor was not a man who required blind faith and obedience. As a matter of fact, questions were not only encouraged, but were expected and respected. The measure of my admiration for him can be gathered from the fact that I was one of few students who did not balk at the requirement to attend Sunday services as part of preparing for confirmation. While I don't recall any of Pastor Bobzien's sermons, I do remember running up the hill to the church each Sunday and wanting to be there.

The pastor of the Lutheran Church in Bad Wiessee, Dr. Naumann, who also led the congregation of the community across the lake from us, was more intellectual and outspoken than Pastor Bobzien. From the time I attended his Sunday services and, shortly thereafter became a member of his confirmation class, I was in awe of him. His approach to the Christian faith was direct and demanding—faith was not based on obedience to a nation, but obedience to God; faith was not passive, faith was action; faith included personal responsibilities. Pastor Naumann didn't seem to be afraid to include unveiled anti-authoritarian comments in his sermons and during our classes. He was a remarkable man! Of course, I was afraid for his safety, because I was sure that his outspokenness would lead him to prison, if not to a concentration camp. However, nothing happened to him while we lived in Bad Wiessee. Years later, after World War II had ended, I had the opportunity to speak with someone who had known Dr. Naumann and I was told that the pastor had survived the Third Reich and had continued preaching. I was greatly relieved.

As I reflect on the months of confirmation classes with Dr. Naumann, I realize that his presence and teaching deeply influenced my life. He did not expect the group of fourteen-year old boys and girls to be instantly religious, but tried to guide us to a deeper understanding of the teachings of Jesus. He spoke with courage and conviction and intimated that a commitment to the Christian faith was to be more than praying and seeking comfort, but required responsible actions on our part. I believe I began to move toward adulthood under his tutelage.

My confirmation in the Bad Tegernsee Lutheran Church, on April 11, 1943, was a significant event in my life and in the St. Josefsheim community. In a letter to my mother I recorded the day in detail:

"The day started with a special breakfast prepared by the nuns, a
bouquet of tulips at my place, along with a special cake. Right after
breakfast I ran into the kitchen to thank the nuns personally—each of
them so loving and kind. After breakfast, most of the class, our teachers
and I, walked to the pier in Bad Wiessee from where two large rowboats
took us across the wind tossed lake to the town of Tegernsee, where I
experienced a most beautiful confirmation service. When it was my
turn to be confirmed the pastor presented me with a certificate showing
an Albert Dürer etching of St. George on his horse and the words of
the thirty-third verse of the Gospel of St. John 16: "*In der Welt habt ihr
Angst; aber seid getrost, ich habe die Welt überwunden!*"—(You will be
afraid in this world, but be consoled, for I have overcome the world.)
I believe Pastor Naumann chose this particular verse for me, because
of the fear of the war, of bombing and Nazism that permeated our
world. Part of the morning's service was Holy Communion—my first
communion. A few days ago, Fräulein Mahlstedt (the English teacher
who had replaced Dr. Dening in early January) explained the meaning
of communion to me—although I still found it difficult to understand.
However, communion was a significant experience and I realized that
I was now a Christian, with all the responsibilities this identification
entails. I want you to know that I quietly prayed and thought about
the life I want to lead, about being honest, kind, and helpful. After the
confirmations of several other local students were completed my classmates sang the '*Te Deum*' as an offering to the whole congregation—it
is such a beautiful hymn. What a service! It was overwhelming! After
the service we went back to Bad Wiessee by rowboat, walked back to
St. Josefsheim, where I was again congratulated by the nuns who had
prepared a holiday dinner for us. After dinner I was led to a table of
gifts—more flowers, poems, letters from family members and friends
in Worpswede and a few books. The whole day had been a celebration!
I was so happy! Before I went to bed that night I went to Fräulein
Cabisius, to Fräulein Mahlstedt, to my fellow students and the nuns
and thanked each of them once more for this beautiful day. And, of
course, many thanks to you, dear Mami, for all you have taught me.

I remain your happy daughter, Christa!"

For years, during my move from Germany to the United States and several moves within the States, I carefully saved the confirmation certificate, which was presented to me on April 11, 1943. However, I misplaced it sometime during the past eight years and was afraid I would never find it again. On April 18, 2005, while looking through some art books, I suddenly discovered the certificate between the pages of one of those books. What a remarkable coincidence! Although the certificate is now yellowed, the edges brittle and small fragments of paper have broken off, the image of the 1508 Albrecht Dürer etching, the handwritten biblical verse, John 16.v.33, the dates of my birth, baptism, and confirmation, as well as the signature of Dr. Naumann, are still intact. I am thankful that this document still exists.

In another footnote to the day of my confirmation I want to share part of a letter Fräulein Cabisius wrote to my mother: "Despite the letter from the authorities in München, which prohibited our girls from participating in the church service—the singing of the *Te Deum*—the students, on their own, decided that they could circumvent the order by stating that they would be singing during their free, unrestricted time on a Sunday morning. Thus, I was able to support their plans with a clear conscience and did not have to fear any repercussions." I cite this as an example of the long arm of the Nazi government, which, generally successful, reached into the smallest crevices of our private lives. But not on the day of my confirmation!

It is personally revelatory to re-read my letter to my mother, dated April 11, 1943, for it discloses the struggles of a fourteen-year old who wants to experience the event of confirmation as a serious young adult, yet remains an exuberant and emotional child. I find further evidence of this inner conflict in letters from my teachers to my mother. One of the letters reads: "...Christa showed a childlike appreciation of what was offered to her on this day of celebration" and "I want to convey to you that today's confirmation was a significant day for our dear Christa; a day, which undoubtedly will remain in her memory as beautiful." In other letters to my mother I am described as "a healthy, unaffected and cheerful girl"—and that is how I remember myself, even though I wanted and tried to be more serious and introverted. I believed that my laughter, enthusiasm, and eager appreciation of what was beautiful in my life were superficial. It continued to be my struggle for several years.

Most of the memories of the remaining weeks in Bad Wiessee— we returned to Bremen in mid-May—have disappeared over the years. The few letters I wrote home between April and early May speak of finishing the school year, packing boxes and preparing for the trip home. However, despite the excitement and joy at the prospect of seeing our families again, a sense of sadness surrounded our small school community as the day of leaving St. Josefsheim and the beautiful mountains drew closer. I know that most of us felt the ache of knowing that we would probably never see the kind nuns again and that we would never be able to repeat the extraordinary experiences of our shared living of the past nine months. This brings to mind a short poem, a gift given to me by one of my classmates on the day of my confirmation. This verse has accompanied me since April 1943:

> *Was vergangen kehrt nicht wieder,*
> *Aber ging es leuchtend nieder,*
> *Leuchtet's lange noch zurück.*

> What has passed will not return,
> But if it vanished with a glow
> It will radiate for a long time.

Most of the schools that had spent nearly a school year in Bad Wiessee returned to Bremen around the middle of May in 1943.

Within weeks classes reconvened in Bremen's girls' high school Karlstrasse and the pre-dawn walks to the train station and dealing with air raids became part of my daily world again. However, within a couple of months, parents and students were notified of a second phase of evacuation due to the ever-increasing intensity of the *Luftkrieg* (aerial war). The school evacuation plans of 1943 stated that students were to be moved to small towns in the state of Thuringia, several hundred miles east of Bremen, and would be housed with individual families. From the day of this announcement I knew that I did not want to participate in this evacuation; not only did I realize that it would be impossible to duplicate the wonderful experience of Bad Wiessee, but I was also uncomfortable at the thought of being assigned to a family that may not have volunteered to house and care for an unknown teenager; or, even worse for me, I could be assigned to a family of staunch Nazis. We were further informed that students would attend local high schools, indicating that none of our teachers would accompany us. My mother agreed with my objections and we looked for another solution to continue my education.

The school dilemma was resolved by the kind offer of Barbara's parents, Mr. and Mrs. Scholvin, who lived in Thedinghausen, a village south of Bremen, that I move into their home and attend the girl's high school in Verden with Barbara. Verden, a provincial city about sixteen miles south of Thedinghausen, had rarely experienced air raids and thus was considered a safe location. I believe it was sometime during August when I moved in with the Scholvin family. Barbara and I continued to be best of friends and, by and large, I enjoyed life at school and at her home, although I was aware that caring for an additional active teenager wasn't always easy on Barbara's mother. I returned to my family in Worpswede each weekend. What do I remember about my weekends with my mother and sisters? Nothing more than the race to the train station after Saturday morning classes in order to catch the only afternoon train to Bremen with a connection to Worpswede; then, early Monday morning, I embarked on the reverse race back to Verden in time for school.

Although I stayed with Barbara's family for only one year, I continued my schooling in Verden until the end of March 1945, a time when most schools closed due to the advancing war throughout Germany. It was kind of the Scholvin family to open their home to me in the summer of 1943; however, when the decision was made that I was not going to live with them during the following school year, I was not surprised, yet felt that I had failed in some way. Was there a specific reason why my stay with the Scholvin family came to an end? Perhaps I was too independent? Perhaps I did not make enough of an effort to fit into the family pattern? I believed I had created some tension within the family circle. Years later, sometime around the mid-fifties, Barbara's mother wrote a thoughtful letter to me, expressing her sorrow that she had not been able to be more accepting of me while I lived with them. At that point in my life, being a mother of four children, I had a deeper understanding of what the daily care and supervision of children involved and responded in kind to her. Whereas Barbara and I had always been able to bridge our differences in upbringing and personality by our genuine friendship, her mother, undoubtedly, was at times overwhelmed by the added responsibility of caring for two active adolescents during the uncertain days of the war.

In the summer of 1944 I briefly lived with an aunt in Bremen while attending school in Verden. The daily round trip between Bremen and Verden was not much of a problem; however, the nightly air raids, which, in addition to the fear meant getting next to no sleep, soon demanded a change. By early fall I was invited to stay in the homes of one or another classmate in and around Verden—a temporary, unsatisfactory solution. It may have been late fall when my mother decided to rent a room for me in Verden, close to the school, where

I lived until our school closed in March of 1945.

Sometime during the last school year in Verden I was aware that my vagabond type of existence was not the norm, not even during wartime. Yet, I somehow managed and felt competent to take care of myself. As I focus on that year, trying to retrieve and assess my reaction to my nomadic life, I question my acceptance of being shuttled around. My apparent consent appears contradictory to the person I was: an individual who questioned authority at all times. I followed Mami's directions as a matter of course—and I don't want to say "orders," because I never thought of orders in terms of my mother. I can only assume that my unshakeable belief in my mother's judgment concerning the importance of school guided me through that year. Knowing that she trusted me to handle difficult situations helped me to cope with the pressures and uncertainties of my school year in Verden, with the war, with Nazism, hunger, and living without family.

Postscript

It seemed nearly impossible that Barbara and I would have a chance to revisit Bad Wiessee, the town that had sheltered us during the school year 1942-43. Yet during a visit with Barbara—it must have been in 2008—while we reminisced about our experiences in Bad Wiessee we decided on the spur of the moment to plan a trip into our past. Thus, a year later, on May 25, 2009, Barbara and I embarked on a long day of traveling by train and bus from her home near Unterlüss in northern Germany to Bad Wiessee, at the foot of the Alps. It was an altogether different journey than the one we had taken with our class and hundreds of other school children in September of 1942. As we traveled through Germany our thoughts turned to our teachers and classmates. Many of them are gone and/or we lost touch with them. Yet on this journey they were present in every way.

When we finally arrived at our stop in Bad Wiessee we walked, with our bags rolling behind us, to the nearest multi-directional street sign to guide us to the *pension* where we were to stay for the next few days. The sign not only indicated how to get to our pension but in addition showed directions to a St. Josefsheim. Could it be OUR St. Josefsheim, the home where we lived during 1942-43? We continued to walk in the direction indicated by the sign and suddenly the house came into view. Yes, it was OUR St. Josefsheim, looking just like we had left it in May of 1943. We felt overwhelmed by our special welcome to Bad Wiessee—the beginning of a series of amazing experiences.

The few days we spent in Bad Wiessee continued to be full of surprises. We re-discovered our old paths along Lake Tegernsee; we found the church where we had taken confirmation classes as well as the church in the town of Tegernsee where I was confirmed. We visited the Catholic Church to which our friend Maria had taken us and walked across the meadow below it that had been covered with wild primroses in early spring. We took a boat across Lake Tegernsee in memory of the long-ago boat trip on the day of my confirmation. We "climbed" to the top of the Wallberg via gondola—the mountain that we had climbed on foot in 1943. Due to spring's late arrival on the Wallberg we discovered a field of primroses at the peak, the same we had picked in the valley more than sixty years ago. Each day was filled with joyful rediscoveries in an unchanged environment— experiences we had not dared to expect when we planned our trip.

My last diary entry of our visit in Bad Wiessee reads as follows: "Reflecting on the adventure of our three days in Bad Wiessee and its surroundings, I am thankful that we were able to reach back into the past and that it did not disappoint us. We visited the places we had hoped to visit. We saw and experienced more than we had anticipated. Not only were we able to retrace our steps of 1942-1943, but we walked the paths with fresh eyes and new understanding."

MY GRANDMOTHER

Margarethe Bölken-Mülller

Reflecting on and writing about my childhood makes me aware how little I know about some of my family members—grandparents, aunts, uncles, and cousins. The gaps in knowledge were not only due to inter- and intra- family separations within the individual Bölken and Meiners families, but also to the physical distance between our small family unit in Worpswede—Mami, Charly, Angela, and I—and our relatives, although many of them lived in Bremen, a city about 20 miles away. In today's society such a short distance would easily be bridged by a less than half-hour car ride and not require more than a moment's decision. However, sixty to seventy years ago a trip between Bremen and Worpswede, generally by train, was more cumbersome and needed planning; hence the trips back and forth were infrequent.

Then, after the start of World War II and the onset of bombing raids, train trips, unless they were essential, became even less frequent. Another factor, which kept us separated was silence—the silence, which obscured the reasons for the disconnection within the extended family. I do not know whether the silence was imposed because my sisters and I were too young to understand the relationships between family members outside our immediate circle or whether my mother intentionally kept family information to a minimum. What is certain is that I have only sketchy knowledge, sometimes no more than the name and a vague outline of a face of persons with whom I shared a legal and genetic relationship. In recent years, knowing that even an absent or seldom seen family member may have a profound impact on one's life, I decided to retrieve and reconstruct my few memories and, in the process, gain insight into how some of my relatives helped shaped my life. One of these persons was my mother's mother, my Großmama— Margarethe Bölken-Müller.

Margarethe Müller was born into a prosperous merchant family in 1880 in Bremen. In the summer of 1900 she married Max Bölken, a Bremen businessman, three years her senior. They had three children: Andree, born in 1901, Juliane (my mother), born in 1903, and Marcus, born in 1905. Shortly after World War I, while my mother was still in her teens, her parents separated. The children stayed with their father. I don't believe that the feelings of rejection my mother experienced when her mother left her and her two brothers in search of a different, independent life were ever resolved. Hence, this broken relationship was passed on to us; not so much in direct conversations as by the tension my sisters and I sensed when Mami, although infrequently, referred to her childhood. I am not sure if I knowingly heard my mother's stories or whether I subconsciously absorbed some of her recollections and secreted them in a memory bank for future retrieval. Indeed, more than five decades passed before those random words and images, along with my own observations and reflections, began to coalesce into a portrait of my mother's mother. At first glance the picture seemed incomplete, because the memories of *Großmama's* visits were few and overshadowed by the recollections of life under Nazism and World War II. Only years later, with the help of my mother's family album, a letter, my grandmother's Bible, and her Spanish-German dictionary, am I ready to attempt to create a tangible likeness of the woman to whom I am related by genes and spirit: Margarethe Bölken-Müller.

The first memory I have of Großmama connects to one of her few visits in Worpswede around the mid nineteen-thirties, when I was six or seven years old. I can still visualize my grandmother, a slight woman with masses of white hair, which were not carefully combed or wound into the customary bun, but surrounded her head like a wreath. She was always dressed in an off-white sweat suit and wore sandals, because, as she explained to us, she preferred loose clothing from top to toe—freedom of movement was essential to her. When she visited us in Worpswede or spent her summers with her son Andree in Bremen, she preferred staying in her tent rather than in our homes—she did not want to be confined by walls. To this day I have a vague recollection of a large white tent, pitched in our front yard or near the apple orchard at my uncle's farm in Bremen. Needless to say, there was not another grandmother in all of Worpswede who lived in a tent while visiting her family; as a matter of fact, I don't think anyone in the village chose to live in a tent rather than a building with four walls. I don't recall how we first learned about our grandmother's preference for living in a tent. No doubt, the idea must have seemed strange at first, but once the tent was pitched in our yard I didn't give it much thought. Looking back, I am amazed at the apparent ease with which Großmama lived outside the bounds of conventions.

With that in mind I recall a summer day when my sisters and I met Großmama at a railroad station about three kilometers from the center of Worpswede—the walk back into town seemed especially long and hot. Großmama, being true to her unconventional self, insisted that we join her in singing and taking deep breaths, along with raising and lowering our arms, while walking toward our village. She told us that the singing and breathing exercises were not only for the sake of good health, but also an expression of jubilance—praising nature, praising the sun, and delighting in the fresh country air. Years later, after reading some of her letters and remembering her exuberance while walking, I realized that affirmation of nature, specifically the sun as life giver, was at the center of her being. However, at our young age my sisters and I did not connect to her philosophical perceptions and worshipful enthusiasm. Instead we slowly trotted behind her, lamely lifting our arms off and on. Did one of us join in her singing? I don't remember. Although we were taught to be respectful toward all adults and would not have considered asking Großmama not to sing and do gymnastics along the way, we must have felt that her public behavior was embarrassing. Today I think that she must have wondered why we didn't have the innocence to follow her freely.

Another memory of that visit is clearly before me; an incident that seemed then and still today to be in complete contradiction to the freedom from convention my grandmother espoused. Early one morning, as Großmama entered our home, I greeted her with the traditional handshake and wishing her *Guten Morgen*, before going into the yard. Within minutes I stepped back into the house, walking past her through the kitchen, to join my sisters at the breakfast table. Suddenly I received a resounding slap on my cheek from my grandmother—along with a few words that expressed her annoyance at my lack of manners by not greeting her again. I was stunned by the slap and her words, believing that my earlier greeting, separated by only the few minutes I spent outdoors, had sufficed. The sting of her slap lasted only a few minutes, but my puzzlement about her contradictory behavior stayed much longer. As the years unfolded, I discovered that Großmama, despite her decidedly non-conformist behavior, at times returned to her traditional upbringing with an uncompromising severity. Even though she defied convention concerning her lifestyle, she never abandoned what she considered "correct manners"—the rigid set of customs, with which she had been brought up.

Early in our childhood Mami spoke to my sisters and me about the concept of eccentricity. I believe my mother instructed us so that we could understand our grandmother's choices, such as her insistence on independence by leaving her husband and children, as well as her subsequent unusual mode of living, her clothing, and strict vegetarian diet. According to Mami, Großmama, emotionally devastated by the violence and killing of the First World War, chose to become a vegetarian before the end of the war. Eventually she extended her avoidance of meat and fish to cooked food—asserting that microbes on vegetables would be killed in the process of cooking. As young children we accepted her as she was, eccentric, but generally not arbitrary, and we understood that her decisions were based on reason. Once World War II started we were able to appreciate her rejection of violence and death, although, at the time, no one in our family chose to become a vegetarian.

In 1986, when my husband Pete and I lived in Tampa, Florida, we hosted a university student from India for a semester. On his first visit to our home we discovered during meal preparation that the young man's religious belief forbade him to eat meat and fish in addition to root vegetables—among them potatoes, carrots, and beets. He explained to us that he and his family were adherents of Jainism, a Hindu sect founded in the 6th century, which emphasizes reverence for all living things, among them the microbes found on root vegetables. During this conversation I suddenly retrieved the memory of my grandmother who would not eat cooked food and realized that the young man's dietary laws were a connection to my grandmother's decision to eat only raw food. Recalling that Großmama had traveled to India in the nineteen-twenties—a journey about which I know very little—I assume that it was in India that she learned about the prac-

Margarethe Bölken Müller in a circle game with her children Andree, Julie and Marcus. Birkenhof, Bremen. Photo by Max Bölken. ca. 1910.

tices of Jainism, a belief that incorporated many of her own ideals.

Despite Großmama's diet of raw food I remember her as being in good health. However, with the onset of World War II, tropical fruits, among them bananas, oranges, pineapples, and certain nuts that had been an important part of her diet, were not as plentiful in the stores as in the pre-war years. Eventually they were not available at all. Therefore, due to restrictions on imports, her choice of foods became increasingly limited with the result that she lost a lot of weight and her general health deteriorated. When, sometime during the summer of 1943, I saw my grandmother for what turned out to be the last time, she looked very thin. In the fall of 1944, shortly after her apartment in Stuttgart had been destroyed during an air raid, Großmama, now dangerously undernourished, was evacuated to a hospital in southern Germany. Efforts by the hospital staff to give her simple nourishment, such as cooked oatmeal that her system might be able to digest, failed and she died within a short time. My mother went to see her in Bavaria shortly before she died. When Mami returned to Worpswede she was sad and silent. She spoke to us about Großmama's death, but I don't recall that she expressed her feelings about losing her mother, which in turn meant that my sisters and I also didn't talk about our feelings. One evening I put a brief note under my mother's pillow, letting her know that I tried to imagine what it felt like to lose one's mother—it was my way of trying to console her, because I was sure she was in pain. I think it was also a way to assuage my feelings of guilt for not experiencing a stronger sense of loss. To this day I regret that my mother did not include us in her mourning, for her silence seemed to say that we didn't have to mourn our grandmother. Unknowingly Mami had given me the message that she had not been important in our lives. Did my mother assume that I interpreted Großmama's infrequent and limited visits as not having taken a serious interest in our lives? Did Mami think that our relationship lacked depth because our grandmother did not sit down with us individually to read or talk or play games with us? As I am retrieving and reliving the few memories of Großmama I realize that more than an individual relationship with her, her honesty, her rejection of violence, and the example of living an unconventional life, have had a significant impact on my development.

There are some specific stories about Großmama, part of family lore, which were handed down to me during my teenage years. There is the incident when, early in World War II, she wrote letters to Hitler, Stalin, Roosevelt and Churchill, chiding them about the war and killing, urging them to resolve their conflicts without arms. The post office handed the letters over to the police and within a day my grandmother was picked up and taken to the police station. Since she was staying with Uncle Andree that summer he was able to intercede on her behalf and persuade the authorities that she suffered bouts of temporary insanity, due to the lingering effects of a sunstroke she had suffered in Italy some years earlier and, therefore, she could not be held liable for her actions. Großmama was remanded to the custody of my uncle and, according to my knowledge, did not attempt to write or at least mail additional letters to politicians. I remember wondering about the sunstroke—when had she been in Italy? Had she really suffered sunstroke or was that an excuse for her action? The expression my uncle had used in describing his mother's condition to the police was *"parzeller Wahnsinn."* It was not clear to me what the expression meant—was it partial insanity, divided insanity, temporary insanity? Could insanity appear on and off? There are a number of gaps in the telling of the letter-writing incident—gaps, which could have been filled by asking my grandmother, but I'm not sure that I knew how to approach the subject. On one level, it was clear to my sisters and me that our grandmother, although eccentric and "different," was saner and showed more courage than most Germans by writing to the world's leaders. We admired her for that. On another level we understood my mother's and Uncle Andree's fear and apprehension about her action. By then we knew that she had exposed herself and the rest of the family to considerable danger—incarceration and worse—by taking pen in hand. However, a rhetorical question remains on my mind: what if all of us had written letters against the war?

It was not until 1988, when my mother gave me the gift of her father's photo album filled with family photos taken during the years 1909 through 1913 that I saw pictures of my grandmother as a young woman—the only pictures of her I have. My grandfather, an early enthusiast of photography, took the photos which beautifully captured his family, his wife and three children, in a series of outdoor and indoor settings. The young Margarethe Bölken, portrayed in elegant poses in their beautiful home and spacious gardens, looks serious and detached, even when surrounded by her children. Perhaps custom and the existing photographic equipment dictated the stiffly held poses of the subjects. Nonetheless it seems strange that mother and children, holding hands and forming a circle, do not give a hint of joy while playing a game together. What is most striking is the fact that the woman I met twenty-five years later seems to have no connection to the woman pictured in the album—not even in physical appearance. Thus the photo album documents Margarethe Bölken, woman, wife, and mother, before her metamorphosis to Margarethe Bölken-Müller—the independent ethereal being of whom no photograph exists.

A gift within the gift—a letter from my grandmother to her husband, Max Bölken—was accidentally found among the empty pages in back of the album. The letter is written in her distinctive handwriting, decorated with a watercolor painting of wild roses. It is a beautiful watercolor, its vibrant shades of red and green remarkably well preserved. The contents of the translated letter convey much about Margarethe Bölken-Müller.

> *Grüss Gott* (Greetings) dear Max.
>
> Summer solstice is approaching and with it, unfortunately, the descent of the sun—I barely felt its strength today. But one must create sun for oneself and, with this in mind, I hope that the watercolor of the roses will bring joy to you.
>
> A black bird is singing outside; with its clear voice and ever-changing rhythm, the bird does not seem affected by the rain and cold.
>
> The bird must be our example so that, despite the hardship of the times, we need to live each day with confidence and joy.
>
> My help comes from closely observing the flowers, especially when I paint and see their indescribable grace and beauty.
>
> I wish you well being and greet you fondly on the twenty-first of June, 1944.
>
> Margarethe

This letter is an unexpected message from the past. From the moment I read the letter I sensed that I had come upon a treasure; a treasure that afforded me insight into my grandmother's world. Her caring words to her husband, from whom she had been separated for close to twenty-five years, express her undiminished concern for him. Her words confirm her love of nature and give voice to her spirit, which, though saddened by war and the absence of sunshine, is renewed by the beauty of a bird's song and the flowers before her. Along with hope I sense a profound sadness in her words—I know her life was filled with both.

Two other gifts from my mother, shedding more light on who Großmama was, were given to me within the last fifteen years—one is my grandmother's Bible, the other the Spanish-German dictionary that she used during her travels in South America. What is significant about the books are the markings that my grandmother made in each—penciled manifestations of what she perceived as significant or repugnant in her life. When I first opened the Bible and saw the many passages she underlined in the Old and New Testament, I realized that she must have read most of the Bible, a remarkable feat in itself. Knowing that she was not religious in the conventional sense of belonging to one faith and one church, I interpret her study of the Bible as a serious search for answers, as well as affirmation in matters of personal faith and ethical living. Among the many sections she underlined are the Ten Commandments and the Lord's Prayer— choices that I understand as her commitment to a spiritual and loving relationship with God and humanity. Seeing the underlined words, "Holy Spirit" and "Resurrection," throughout the New Testament, remind me of her radiant spirituality and her aura of not being confined to her physical environment.

My grandmother also left her mark on the dictionary. The first time I flipped through the pages of the book, I had to chuckle at her determination to stamp out violence, power, and killing by the simple act of crossing out words. The marked dictionary, inscribed with her name, place, and date of purchase in Spanish: "*este libro es comprado en Stuttgart—Junio 13, 1936, de Margarete Bölken-Müller*," became her companion during several trips to South America, mainly Chile, where she visited her youngest son Marcus, who had settled in Santiago sometime during the mid-twenties. A few, fragmented stories of Großmama's life in Chile, her discovery of people living in abject poverty under bridges and in shacks and her attempts to help slum dwellers by buying fruits, soap, and new clothes for them have been handed down to me.

The powerful, cumulative experiences of her travels in India and then in Chile led to her acute awareness of violence, poverty, and isolation based on class, from which she had been shielded during her youth and early adulthood. I believe that by the time my grandmother visited South America, she may have decided that she could be an agent of transformation in the lives of society's outcasts. However, according to the memories of Chilean relatives, her efforts to cross cultural and traditional barriers by her very presence, by her sincerity and compassion, did not bring about the results she had hoped for. There is no record on how she reacted to the failed attempts to change the lives of poor families, but I can imagine that she was disappointed and sad. I think we can safely assume that Großmama had a large capacity for empathy with people who lived in conditions of poverty and injustice. Thus it must have been painful for her to accept that the way out of hopelessness could not be achieved by determination, compassion, and a few material gifts, while at the same time her universal love, *agape*, for the unnamed many could not lead to the peaceful and just world she envisioned.

The highlighted words in the dictionary do not allude to Groß-mama's disappointments in South America, but they tell a story of their own. It is the story of her strong opposition to any form of violence, oppression and injustice as well as her universal belief in the need for peace and respect among people. Decisive pencil strokes are made through such words as battle, butcher and butchering, servitude, police, defense, military service, enemy, and hitting. By contrast she makes small check marks and circles next to such words as trust, peace, love, friendly, enchanting, salvation, breathing, and thinking. I try to imagine what my grandmother thought of as she went through the dictionary with pencil in hand. I don't believe she saw herself as an instrument of censorship; rather her pencil marks appear to me as proof of her elemental belief that peaceful living was not possible while institutions of coercion and force, as well as individual acts of violence continued to exist.

I am thankful for the few pieces of memorabilia of my grand-mother's, for they have established a bond with the woman who, upon reflection, has been a stronger influence in my life than my mother, my sisters and I could have anticipated. I don't think I was aware of this kinship until I struggled to define myself in terms of independent political thinking, in speaking out for universal peace and justice and against all forms of discrimination and oppression.

Throughout the decades since her death I've become increasingly aware of the loss of not having had the chance to get to know Margarethe Bölken-Müller better, not only as my grandmother but also as another woman. Opportunities were lost because of the pained relationship between my mother and her mother; because of the war and the distance between Stuttgart and Worpswede; because Großmama chose to live outside of conventional bounds and I, as a child, was too absorbed in my own small world and did not enter hers. Yet, the past few weeks of concentrated reading, remembering, and reflecting on the life of my grandmother have enabled me to create a narrative portrait of Margarethe Bölken-Müller—for myself and succeeding generations. For that I am thankful.

Gloomy day on the moor. Photo by JMB. ca. 1940.

MY FATHER, CARL OTTO MEINERS
Memories and Reflections

"What about your father?" "Why don't you ever mention your father?" "Didn't he impact your life?" When my professor and fellow students at Bowdoin College raised these questions in 2000 during discussions of our individual histories they didn't mean much to me. I wasn't even aware of the fact that I had left my father out of the story of my childhood. How could I weave him into my early memories when he didn't have a presence in my life until I was nearly ten years old? For that matter, his presence continued to be sporadic even after our re-acquaintance. Had I purposely avoided incorporating my father into the writing of my history because he had ignored me? Did I perceive his influence as too insignificant for inclusion? My responses to their questions were brief and to the point—enough to satisfy their and my curiosity.

However, months later I decided to consider and address these questions to myself in more depth—a process that led me to acknowledge his impact on my life for the simple reason that he was my biological father. Then, as an extension of admitting our physical connection, I knew I had to go further and examine whether we ever developed a father-daughter relationship despite the obvious handicaps we faced from the start. There was still another question before me: what can I say about his persona, his values and character, when I had so few opportunities to observe him while I lived in Germany? Since I rarely experienced my father on a day-to-day basis, I have had to rely on fragments of memories, on overheard conversations and assumptions to portray the dimensions of a man to whom I was connected by genes, by filial respect, and a good measure of ambivalence. However, once I made up my mind to concentrate on the search of memories I found a surprising amount of material to start writing a portrait of my father—*Papi* to me and my sisters.

When I think about Papi it is his absence that first comes to mind. My parents' marriage ended in divorce sometime during the summer of 1931 and it wasn't until his reappearance in the fall of 1938 that my father had a physical presence in our life. He never visited us for seven years. I don't recall any cards or letters, not on birthdays, not at Christmas, during that time. My father may have corresponded with our mother, but she never spoke of it. My sisters and I knew we had a father, just like our friends had fathers, but ours wasn't with us. Since I was less than three years old when my parents separated and, according to my sisters, Papi was often away on business during our parents' seven years of marriage, it is not surprising that he never became a strong figure in the world of my childhood.

Am I able to recall any specific events in my early years, which made me conscious of missing him? Although I have carefully and repeatedly searched my memory I cannot recollect one particular instance when I felt any loss at his absence. If this brief statement concerning the years without Papi sounds cold-hearted, indicting both of us on different levels, it is not to be understood in that way. As I retrieve the memories of my earliest childhood, I am aware of having felt sheltered and happy within my immediate family—my mother, my sisters and our live-in housekeeper Hille. In addition, we were surrounded by an extended family of caring friends and neighbors, both artists and farmers. Apparently, not having a father at home didn't mean that I considered my family incomplete.

Despite my father's presence during the earliest years of my life I have retained only shadowy memories of living with him, memories most likely reinforced by later occasional family conversations. Specifically, I remember two incidents pre-dating my parents' separation. My first recollection of Papi appears unclear, like a fuzzy photograph, yet not an illusion. My sisters later confirmed that I was only about two and a half years old the evening my father was left with his three young daughters while Mami and Hille had gone out to see a movie. We lived in Erfurt at the time, a city in central Germany. Papi, who was a fun-loving person and liked to play jokes—*er war ein Spassmacher (jokester)*—encouraged us to help him barricade the front door with mattresses from our beds, so that Mami and Hille would have a difficult time getting back into the house. I remember sitting on one of the mattresses as Papi and my sisters pulled and pushed it down the hallway toward the door. It was a hilarious situation and we were laughing, falling all over ourselves; we were having a great time with our father. However, when Mami and Hille returned they did not think barricading the door was amusing. I vaguely recall their pounding on the front door and I visualize my mother's surprised and exasperated face when Papi finally pushed the mattress aside and opened the door. With that picture in my mind the memory fades.

Another, more distinct remembrance, in stark contrast to the incident in Erfurt, takes me to Worpswede, the community that became our home in the summer of 1931. Papi was in town for what was likely his last visit until the summer of 1938. On a Sunday morning Mami sent Charly, Angela, and me to visit Papi in his rented room in a pension in the center of the village. It must have been quite early, because when we went to his room we found him still asleep in his bed. Which of my sisters suggested that one of us should put a wet sponge on my father's face in order to wake him up? Perhaps both of them concocted the idea. In any case, I was chosen to be the one to tiptoe to his bed and touch his forehead with the cold sponge. Papi woke up with a start and didn't seem happy about being awakened by cold water dripping on his face. The father, whom I only remembered as being playful and full of mischief, was annoyed by the trick we played on him. Papi's reaction startled me; I believe it was a response that none of us had expected.

With that visit Papi disappeared from our lives. I do not remember that we talked about him nor do I remember seeing a picture of him. Did my sisters and I miss Papi? Most likely we did. However, the transition from living with two parents to one parent must have gone smoothly, because I don't recall any abrupt changes. As far as I can remember, my sisters and I continued to feel secure.

Papi returned to Worpswede in July or August of 1938. I assume that Mami told us about his impending visit and his wish to take us on a vacation at the seashore several days before he arrived. I remember that Angela and I were excited about meeting our father and we speculated what he might look like—after the seven years of his absence we did not remember his face. It is likely that Charly had met Papi sometime earlier, because she didn't join in our excitement and speculations yet didn't offer any information. Angela and I didn't think that he would look like any of the fathers in Worpswede. Papi was a stranger to us and we assumed that he would have to look very different from any of the fathers we knew. Would he look like the traveling salesman who, with a suitcase full of small treasures, occasionally came to Worpswede and sold his wares from house to house?

The day arrived when Mami walked with us to the center of the village where we awaited the arrival of our estranged father. We were standing on the sidewalk when Papi suddenly drove up in a car. Angela and I were amazed. Few people beside the doctor and the pastor in Worpswede owned a car. I don't remember anything about greeting our father or taking a good look at him. I only remember that, after a brief good-bye to our mother, we climbed into Papi's car and drove off with him to the North Sea. In retrospect I'm surprised that we didn't have any reservations about going on vacation with him. How did Angela and I make this quick transition from waiting for a stranger to accepting Papi as a father? I can only assume that we trusted our mother, who must have given us a sense of confidence about this man who, some years ago, had been part of our life. During the trip to the seashore my sisters and I quickly felt at ease with Papi. We recognized that he was still the person whom we remembered as playful and lighthearted. We enjoyed our weekend vacation with him—staying in a hotel, taking our meals in restaurants, diving into the crashing waves of the North Sea, playing in the white sand and building sand castles. Those were wonderful and new experiences for three children who had grown up far from the ocean. However, I also recall a sense of caution and uncertainty while we were getting reacquainted with Papi. Lacking the normal experiences of growing up with a father, not knowing him within the context of day-to-day family life, had created a gap that couldn't be bridged during those few days.

After this initial vacation Papi visited us more often, perhaps four or five times a year, whenever a business trip took him from Berlin to northern Germany. What I remember most about those first visits was his sense of humor and how well he got along with children. It wasn't long before our friends would tag along on our walks with Papi. Playing hide-and-seek with him was a highlight for everyone in the neighborhood. After a couple of years Papi brought his two young daughters from his second marriage, Carla and Heidi, along on his visits to Worpswede. While Mami's welcoming and friendly attitude toward them played a significant role in our relationship with them, we also knew that Mami's conduct was part of a deeply ingrained code of behavior with which she had grown up and passed on to us. Although Charly, Angela and I accepted the girls as young friends and were protective of them, we weren't able to develop a sister-to-sister connection for many years. We hardly knew our father and we knew our half-sisters even less. Also, we were growing up worlds apart—they lived in the cosmopolitan city of Berlin, while we were growing up in a village.

I've often asked myself who was this man, the father of five daughters, who had abandoned three of them for a number of years and then re-entered their lives, attempting to close the gap created by his absence with his charisma and laughter? What were some of the complexities of this man who was playful and had an enormously curious mind; a man who seldom seemed worried about the future and was able to fulfill his needs and dreams by charming people along the way? Through occasional conversations I learned that Papi, like my mother, had grown up in comfortable circumstances in the city of Bremen. After high school he had read the law, and, following in the footsteps of his father, prepared for a career as a corporate lawyer, although he was much more interested in physics than the intricacies of law. I believe it was sometime during the thirties, when, with a minimum of formal scientific studies, he proclaimed himself an engineer. Actually, he was an inventor, a man full of ideas; a man backed up by his interest in physics and electricity who insisted that well-directed light would eventually bring major benefits to industry, libraries, and homes.

Papi's first invention was an improvement on a "miner's lamp," the light affixed to the helmet of a coal miner. His invention was based on rearranging mirrors in the lamp, creating a more focused light, which, in turn, assured more visibility and greater safety for the miners. After the start of World War II my father developed a street lamp that provided adequate ground light for pedestrians during the dark nights of the blackout, but could not be seen beyond a certain height, thus making it practically invisible to bombers circling overhead. His major inventions after the war found application in England. One of them was a light for commercial weavers; it consisted of the installation of a small light within the shuttle that could easily identify a broken thread. Another invention was a "fog light," a useful tool for the boat traffic on the Thames River; a light which could to some extent penetrate the infamous "London fog." However, Papi's main interest throughout all his working years focused on trying to bring the best possible light, approximating daylight, through a combination of fluorescent and incandescent lighting into homes, libraries, and offices. He believed that good light was not only essential in terms of protecting sight, but also for the general health and psychological well-being of humans that, in turn, would lead to higher productivity. It was this latter approach that eventually brought him acknowledgement within the scientific community—as well as financial success for himself and his family.

Although Papi's early inventions were widely applied, they seldom guaranteed more than a brief relief from financial stress. In part this was due to his not being a careful businessman. My father was a dreamer. His interest lay in the inventions themselves, not in marketing them. The partnerships he formed, except for an English firm with which he was associated for a number of post-World War II years, were seldom well managed because he attracted people who had ideas and dreams rather than business sense. Was he ever discouraged by the lack of a steady income? I'm not certain. However, I do know that the lack of financial success never deterred him from continuing with experimentation and refinement of his inventions throughout his long life. In slow times he studied history and literature and seemed to ignore much of the day-to-day financial difficulties his second family had to deal with. Not only was Papi raised in a well-to do family in Bremen where money was not an issue, but he grew up in a time period when it was unheard of to discuss money within the family circle. Yet I presume that it was not only the credo of his family, but also his pride, which prevented him from acknowledging that his financial circumstances differed from those of his youth.

I believe Papi's financial instability and an apparent lack of interest in money per se was the major reason for my parents' divorce. The vague comments handed down to me from my sisters pointed toward my mother's unwillingness to live with financial uncertainty, especially when there were three young children to be fed and clothed. Yet it may have been her father's ultimatum that he would not continue to support the family of an irresponsible dreamer, a man who chose to concentrate on his ideas instead of his familial responsibilities that was decisive. My mother never elaborated on her brief marriage until much later in life. Perhaps she had spoken to my sisters in earlier years, but since I was far from home as of age nineteen, my mother didn't speak to me of her marriage until my own children were grown. I remember her saying that she had loved her husband, my father, very much and that the early separation had been very painful for her. She also inti-

My father, Carl Otto Meiners. Photo by JMB. 1946.

mated at that time that his charm and liveliness had led him to brief liaisons with other women. I don't doubt that those circumstances also contributed to her decision to divorce her husband.

The above paragraphs are but a brief outline of what I heard about my father during my pre-teen and teen years. From the day of our re-acquaintance I frequently thought about the impact our father had on us despite our not living together. Would our lives change now that we had met him? However, it didn't take long for my sisters and me to realize that Papi could only be a "half-father" to us. Without a doubt his major responsibilities rested with his younger, second family. Yet while I knew that he would not be able to give me the time and attention of a full-time parent I appreciated him as an intelligent and interesting person. My father was a curious and witty individual and I selfishly hoped that I had inherited some of these traits. Unfortunately, he wasn't able to share much of himself during those early years of our re-acquaintance and, due to time constraints, our relationship remained superficial—having fun, playing and laughing together. Although I wanted to ask Papi questions about politics and the inner and outer turmoil created by Nazism and the war, there was never enough time of a quiet space for such conversations. I don't recall sharing any thoughtful moments with him until many years later.

For instance, I was very interested in the development of the "black-out" street lamps he had invented—the dimmed light shed on streets and sidewalks that could not be detected by bombers. On the one hand I was proud to have a father who was an inventor and had donated several of the "black-out" street lamps to Worpswede. On the other hand, I felt uncomfortable about this invention because it aided the German "war effort," even though the safety created was primarily for pedestrians. I know that I can safely assume that Papi was anti-Nazi; he was not a nationalist, never wore a party button and clearly opposed the Nazi philosophy. Yet I wondered then and still wonder who funded his scientific research and the development and production of the street lamps. It was obvious that his invention was only applicable during a war. Therefore, its funding source had to be connected to the Nazi government.

There is another unresolved question on my mind. It may have been sometime during 1941 when Papi sent brand new pairs of figure skates to Angela and me—Charly didn't care for sports. We loved the skates. They were beautiful and fashionable shoe skates, much easier to put on than our old skates, which we had to fasten to our boots with leather straps. Mami told us that Papi had sent the skates from Norway. What was my father doing in Norway during a time when Germany occupied the country? Even though I was uncomfortable about the origin of the skates I never shared my concerns with my mother or sisters. It was too awful to think that Papi worked for the Nazi government. Furthermore, although I felt guilty about the skates, I loved rushing across the ice-covered river and flooded meadows with them and I was not willing to give them up. Within two years I had outgrown both Angela's and my pair; the magic and the guilt were gone, although remembered to this day.

When I was twelve years old Papi began to send a monthly allowance to Charly, Angela and me. In some way this gesture changed my relationship with him for I must have seen the monthly allowance as a sign of his being more committed to us; it was a token which told me that he thought of us on a regular basis. Since it was the first time I had received an allowance the event has stayed on my mind. Along with the money—one mark per month—Papi sent a small account book to each of us in which we had to write down the kind and cost of each of our purchases. My little book listed cupcakes and cinnamon rolls at ten pennies each along with such items as an occasional pencil, a notebook or an eraser, month after month. As I am visualizing the day when the first allowance and the account book arrived, I am wondering if it was Papi who sent the small book, because I grew up with the idea that he was rather casual with money. Most likely it was Mami who added the account book for she wanted us to be aware on what we spent our allowance.

Suddenly I'm aware of another memory of Papi—an example of an unexpected commitment to me. One day, during the two years I attended the girls' high school in the town of Verden, Papi came to the school to meet with the headmaster and some of my teachers. I was completely surprised when I met him at my school—perhaps in a hallway?—for no one had told me of his visit. I remember that I was not doing well in some of my classes and perhaps my mother had urged my father, while on a business trip in the area, to accept the responsibility of meeting with the school administration on my behalf. My father's presence and concern puzzled me, because he had never become involved in our lives beyond the occasional friendly visits at home.

I don't remember that Papi admonished me after having met with the school officials and teachers or that he spoke to me about my study habits. I also don't remember whether I improved in my classes after his visit—all I remember is my utter astonishment that he had taken the time to come to Verden to see my teachers. I don't doubt that our father took an interest in my sisters and me beyond the few instances I am recording here; however, I don't recall him as a parent who was anxious about his children's intellectual development. I believe he assumed that our family background was sufficient guarantee of a certain level of intelligence and future accomplishments. I don't think that anxiety was ever a part of our father's make-up—at least I wasn't aware of it. He always seemed sure that life would take its course and everything would turn out all right in the end.

Was Papi able to apply this philosophical stance to the reality of facing hunger during the war? My father, a tall and strong man, seemed always hungry once the war started. Ration cards could not supply the necessary amount of food for most people and it was not unusual that families ran out of coupons before the reissue of monthly allotments. Whenever Papi came to Worpswede my mother worried if we had enough food to share with him. A slice of bread that we had learned to eat slowly, would disappear in his mouth in a few bites. Of course, no one spoke about this, because it was sad and embarrassing to see him so famished and gulp his food.

Papi and his family were evacuated to the provincial city of Oldenburg in northern Germany a few months before the end of World War II—they were considered refugees, *Flüchtlinge*. Oldenburg, a mid-sized city, about fifty miles west of Bremen, was seldom bombed. For the remainder of the war they lived in relative safety. Although our father now lived much closer to us he seldom visited. It was a safety issue. Trains were often targets of machine gun attacks by low-flying aircraft during the last months of the war; therefore, travel by train—I know that Papi had given up his car some years earlier, because gas for personal use was not available any longer—was a risk one had to consider carefully.

In early 1946, less than a year since the war had ended, I visited my father and his second family in Oldenburg. It was my first opportunity to meet Papi's wife, Yvonne. There was no strangeness in our meeting. Yvonne welcomed and accepted me as easily as Mami had accepted Carla and Heidi some years ago, perhaps with even less formality. However, seeing Papi as an integral part of a family was a strange experience for me. When he had visited us in Worpswede he had remained an outsider, not only because he always stayed at a local pension and we would only see him for a few hours each day, but primarily because he never assumed the position of a father. Was it because Mami, even though she never appeared to me as possessive, would not let him take that role? In Oldenburg I saw Papi function as a father and husband. I saw that he was no longer a bystander, but that he belonged and participated in the day–to-day activities of his family. There was a sense of ease about Papi that I had never seen before.

In June of 1947 I left Germany for the United States. I had met my future husband, an American soldier named Peter DeTroy, in the spring of 1946. The following spring, after Pete had returned to the States, we became engaged and I began the lengthy process of acquiring the necessary papers to be allowed to join him in America. By mid-June everything was in place and my departure was set for late June. Our family was spread out at that time—Mami and Angela were still in Worpswede, Charly was living and working in Bremerhaven, Papi was living in Oldenburg and I was working in Oberammergau, in southern Germany. We agreed that we would meet in Frankfurt, the city of my departure, for a couple of days of visiting before my flight to New York City. Thus, my family—my mother, my sisters Charly and Angela, and even my father—met me in Frankfurt on June 24th for a brief reunion. It was both a happy and a painful time. I was not quite nineteen years old and I know it was difficult for my family to let me leave for a country far away; to join a family that, except for Pete, was unknown to all of us. No doubt my parents—and at that moment I considered them a unit—agonized whether they were acting responsibly in letting their youngest child go out into an unfamiliar world, a world not just separated by a long train ride from our home, but separated from Worpswede by a vast ocean. Did the unknown frighten me? Not at all! I loved my family and I wanted to spare them heartache and worry, but I was also self-centered and in love and I wanted to be with Pete. As I recall the moment before I boarded the bus to the airport, I see all of us standing in a circle: my mother looks calm and loving, not saying one word about her pain, her doubts and worries; my father looks a little helpless, not sure whether he could or should offer some fatherly advice; my sisters smile at me; then, from one moment to the next, they cry. We embrace silently before I enter the bus. Next I am standing at the open window of the moving bus, waving good-bye to my whole family—my mother, my father and my two sisters. My last thought, which was probably on their minds as well: would we ever see each other again?

In the ensuing years, I became acquainted with my father through the medium of writing. Despite the fact that I did not return to Germany for twenty-seven years and my father was not able to visit me during those years, our exchange of letters enabled us to get to know each other better than we ever did during his occasional visits in my childhood and youth. Our letters provided the necessary means with which to express our thoughts and interests; we "conversed" about our families, about literature and history, and about the different worlds in which we lived. From the day I arrived in the United States, June 25th 1947, until now, winter of 2003/2004, our family has exchanged lengthy weekly letters. My mother and my sisters sent me a weekly family letter, relating the daily events and experiences of their lives in Worpswede and, as of July 1949, in Chile. My weekly letters to them described not only my new life in the States, but also became a geography lesson of sorts as Pete, our growing family and I moved to several different states around the country. The correspondence between my father and me was not as frequent, but my mother often forwarded copies of my letters to him. Papi and I shared our lives as never before.

Since the nineteen-seventies and eighties Charly, Angela and I, and some of our children and their families, have individually visited our father and Yvonne in Füssen, a resort town in the German Alps, which became their home in the summer of 1965. The hours I spent talking with Papi were extraordinary. Finally we had the opportunity to cement and expand our written "conversations" of the previous years on a one-to-one basis. Papi, by then semi-retired, was generous with his time as he clearly enjoyed getting to know me better. He liked to take walks, always stopping at a restaurant for a glass of beer or soda midway in our excursions; he enjoyed a quiet pause and the chance to rest. It gave both of us a chance to reflect on our conversation and share further insights or commentary on the way home. Papi's special joy was to get to know his grandchildren, questioning them about their interests and hopes; thoughtfully responding to them within a framework of history and literature. Their grandfather fascinated the younger generation.

When I visited Papi I also took time to get to know Yvonne and my sister Carla, who also lived in Füssen, better. We enjoyed walking and hiking in the lower hills of the Alps. Yvonne never tired of showing us special paths, trees, and flowers—that was her passion. Although I probably didn't visit my father and Yvonne more than six times during the late seventies and into the eighties, the memory of the time and conversations we shared is very strong. Getting to know my father on an even plane, adult-to-adult, was an unexpected experience; we appreciated each other.

Recently I discovered some of my father's letters and I spent several days re-reading them. The first letter is dated August 17th, 1947, less than two months after my departure from Frankfurt. Papi begins his letter by wishing me all the best for my birthday on September 22nd. Seeing the mid-August mailing date recalls that mail between Germany and the United States took at least one month to reach its destination during the post-war years. I don't think that airmail was available in Germany at that time—perhaps it was too expensive; it certainly was not common. In his first post-war letter Papi tells me about the continued food shortages and hunger; ration cards were still used and they were as insufficient then as they had been during the war. My father writes about his perception that present day society was returning to the days when the man and father of a household had to be a hunter, capturing wild animals in order to feed his family. He writes: "It is not enough to earn money or to have a position which gives you respect—no, the success of a man rests entirely on his ability to feed his family. Therefore I have decided to concentrate only on my family and not to worry about my business with the mining companies, because they cannot give me any food." He goes on: "I am pained when your sister Angela calls me from Worpswede with her worries about food. I wish I were strong enough to be able to provide for her household as well." The theme of hunger and the inability to provide foodstuffs recurs in most of his early letters.

My father also addresses his feelings about my having emigrated to the United States. He writes: "By and large I am happy that you have married overseas, because a German, as I already saw it after Germany's defeat in World War I, is more than ever a person immersed in his problems. Aside from the influence of winning or losing a war, I believe the "New World" has a different, a less complicated outlook on life and it is enough for me to know that you love Pete and that he is a loving and responsible husband." As I read this letter, more than fifty years after it was written, I am struck by his ability to expand his personal concern for me within a broad perspective. I also reflect on his use of the words "responsible husband," since Papi had generally been presented to me as an irresponsible person.

Through our correspondence I also became acquainted with my grandmother, my father's mother. I think it was in the fall of 1950, after our second child, Gregory, was born, that I decided to ask my father for her address. I remember thinking that it seemed wrong to keep our children, my grandmother's great-grand children, ignorant of each other. Certainly, we could not afford the journey to Germany, but we could visit via letters and with photos. To this day I am thankful that I had the sense to open our communication, because it was a joy to my grandmother and to me; it also enabled me to get to know my father within the context of his early environment.

My father's family had been a large, comfortably situated family, apparently typical in terms of traditional values and solidity. However, Papi's family was also rent by war, by death and emigration, by the German economic collapse during the twenties, and finally by divorce. My father had four brothers and three sisters; one of his brothers died as a small child, two of them were killed during World War I, one emigrated to Brazil in the early thirties and never returned home for a visit. Of his sisters the youngest, Eva, is still alive—she will be 91 years old this year. Lisa, the only aunt I met during her brief visit to Worpswede during the early forties, died of cancer at age 43. His other sister lived into her eighties. My grandmother, Marie Meiners, neé Gildemeister, was divorced from her husband, Herman Meiners, sometime during the thirties. Both remarried shortly after their divorce. My grandmother married Ludwig v. Vallade, who became a sort of honorary great-grandfather to our children, often adding his regards and signature to my grandmother's letters. My grandfather, Herman Meiners, married a woman with the first name of Verena. I met both of them briefly after World War II, but we never established a relationship. Perhaps it was too late.

In the summer of 1964 my grandmother (she was ninety-three years old at the time) sent me a letter that to this day moves me deeply. Peter, our oldest son, spent the summer of 1964 in Germany as a member of an exchange program for high school juniors. During the eight weeks' program in the town of Krefeld Peter was able to spend a long weekend with his grandfather—my father—and travel with him to the town of Much, where my grandmother lived at the time. My grandmother's letter is an expression of sheer joy about meeting Peter, a representative of the American Meiners family. She writes most touchingly of the day when Peter and Papi left to return to Peter's school in Krefeld: "Peter was so charming as he was leaving, saying *"Auf Wiedersehen"* (I'll see you again) to me and I know that he honestly meant it. It would be so wonderful if I could see him again." My grandmother died in the fall of the following year.

I've saved dozens of Papi's letters. Most of them are written in the months of August or December, to congratulate me on my September birthday and to wish Pete, me and our increasing brood of children, a Joyful Christmas (*Fröhliche Weihnachten*) and a Happy New Year (*Glückliches Neujahr*). Along with Papi's wishes for us he inserts information about his professional life, such as his invention of the shuttle light for the weaving industry. It is clear that he had much more success with his inventions after the restructuring of the German currency. He writes of his travels to London, of attending a scientific fair in Brussels, of giving lectures in Sweden and Egypt. Absent are the worries about food and safety. Each of his letters addresses his interest in history and literature and his search for insight into world-wide movements and events. Yes, he was a reader and thinker, but I realize that he selected his reading material carefully. In contrast to his fascination and enthusiasm for the expansion of modern scientific knowledge, he shied away from modern literature and recent books on history and philosophy. It appears to me that Papi's apprecia-tion of ideas and concepts rested on the basis of their compatibility with his opinions, which were formed as a young man of privileged background. This leads me to look at another contradiction in his life: the fact that he never became a financial success did not lead him to abandon a certain elitism and passive support of the idea of a plutocracy. On the contrary, Papi never had any use for socialism and interference by government in the spheres of business. My sisters and I have often jokingly called him "the last of the plutocrats." Although my father generally enjoyed a sense of humor, we never expressed this characterization in his presence. I believe it could have generated a repeat of the wet sponge event in the summer of 1931.

Rereading his letters from August of 1947 until March of 1993, a few months before his death, has been a remarkable experience. His letters afford me travel through his time and space, as he writes not only of family events and his career journey with style and a fine sense of humor, but interjects recollections of his youth, sharing information about his parents, siblings and relatives, within the context of historical events and customs. His recollections are often touching, such as his repeated mention of the carefree days Charly, Angela, and I spent with him during our vacation trip to the North Sea in the summer of 1938. I now understand those lines as his acknowledgement that his long absence from us, for whatever reason, had been painful for him. I'm sorry that I can't tell him now that it's all right. His letters also make me laugh, because his descriptions of certain experiences, always with a touch of exaggeration, are humorous and vivid.

There is so much that I want to convey about my father—a man who coped with his strengths and weaknesses as best as he could. I know that he never meant to harm or neglect anyone, least of all the people he loved—and that includes my mother. Growing up in a large family may have contributed to a certain selfishness on his part, insisting that he be recognized for his own sake, not only as another father and provider, but as a human being with intelligence, hopes, and dreams. His wish to see his dreams, his inventions, respected and accepted is a repeated theme in his letters. My father was in his mid-sixties when he finally made contact with other international light specialists who affirmed his research on the significance of light on human health. Among my father's letters I have found brochures and excerpts of his articles and lectures, in both German and English, on what became known as "Original Meiners-Kombileuchtung"—the combination of natural and artificial light.

I don't know if anyone within his two families ever understood the depth and intensity of his commitment to scientific insights and progress. Caring and providing for his family was certainly one of

119

his priorities, yet his life was focused on intellectual pursuits rather than traditional success. The process of creative thinking, the search for technical resolutions and, finally, the proof of the validity and usefulness of his inventions, were at the heart of his being. Of course, personal recognition, improving the lives of others, and financial security were also part of his aspirations. In retrospect we, his daughters, marvel at the energy and inventiveness of Carl Otto Meiners, but we are also aware that our father, driven by creative impulses, was not able to serve "two masters" at the same time and that he chose to spend his energy on science rather than on his families. It was left to some of his grandchildren, specifically my son Daniel, to appreciate the inventor, the man of ideas, without any reservations. During a period of five years Daniel lived within a two-hour train ride from my father, enabling him to visit Papi on a regular basis. Daniel, as an electrical engineer, was able to follow and respect the intricacies of my father's inventions due to his own professional training. In addition, the two men were comfortable with each other, knowing that their expectations of each other would not be complicated by filial demands, but were able to focus on the genuine joy of compatibility, mutual interest, and admiration.

In March of 1993, a few months before Papi's death at the age of ninety-four, he wrote a final letter to my sisters and me. In this letter he speaks of his fatigue and his lessening intellectual powers. Yet he had not lost his sense of humor and vividly describes the antics of his deaf great-aunt Meta Plump-Gildemeister—she lived to be one hundred and four years old—who, oblivious of the noise of horse-drawn coaches, would imperiously cross the street when it suited her, causing many near accidents. Then, with the advance of streetcars, Tante Meta refused to accept the fact that she couldn't just step off the moving streetcar when it had reached her house. "Tante Meta was an original," writes Papi. "As children we loved it when she came to dinner, she was very amusing." In closing, my father observes that writing has become difficult for him and that he is hardly able to read the words he has written. He writes that he has given up on his favorite pastime: reading. "I don't need to read anymore, I don't need to see things. Hearing is seeing!" He ends his letter by writing: "My diversion is remembering my long life—my childhood—Bremen—my travels—and all of you, my loved ones, including grandchildren and great-grandchildren!" The letter is signed: "Affectionately, Papi."

When the news of Papi's death on July 13th, 1993, reached me I mourned for the dreamer, the charmer, the intellectual, and the wit. Although we had developed a loving and respectful relationship over the years, it was not based on a traditional father-daughter bond. In the days after his death I took time to reflect on what we had meant to each other: two persons who eventually overcame the distance of time and space through correspondence and a few face-to-face visits; two persons who appreciated one another for our common genetic and cultural inheritance; two persons who did not dwell on regrets, but were grateful for the gifts of enthusiasm and curiosity we shared.

Within a couple of weeks of Papi's death I received a copy of his obituary from my sister Heidi. Strangely, the obituary only listed the family members of the deceased as Yvonne, Papi's wife, our sisters Carla and Heidi and their families, Papi's sister Eva, and a brother-in-law, Erich Trunz, who had been married to Papi's late sister Annemarie. There was no mention of Charly, Angela, and me. I was shocked and surprised, not only because our existence had apparently been denied, but because of my emotional response to the omission of our names. It was painful to have been erased as members of the Meiners family. When, at a later date, I spoke with Heidi about the incomplete obituary and asked her why our names had been omitted, she sounded embarrassed and fumbled with an evasive, unsatisfactory answer. I was embarrassed for Heidi and decided not to pursue the emotional issue. When, at a later date, Charly, Angela and I talked about our exclusion in the obituary, we agreed that we did not want to challenge Heidi, Carla or their mother Yvonne. Perhaps the empty spaces in the obituary symbolized the fact that Papi had never been a member of our "family," just as Charly, Angela, and I had never become part of his "family?" I think this explanation is enough.

JULIE MEINERS-BÖLKEN
IN WORPSWEDE.

When I think of my mother, Julie Meiners-Bölken, "Mami" to my sisters and me, I see her not only as an individual, but also as an integral part of the landscape and surroundings of the village of Worpswede, an artist community in Northern Germany, which was our home from my early childhood into my late teenage years. The picture that instantly comes to mind is Mami with her Leica slung over one shoulder, walking between the grain fields that cover the gentle slope of the Weyerberg. My sisters and I are following her on the wide paths, which remain so familiar to me. Even today, more than sixty years since I left Worpswede, I am able to retrace them without a moment's hesitation. On our long ago walks, usually on Sundays and in all seasons, Mami would stop periodically in order to take photographs of fields, of trees and small woods. Before taking a picture, she would look skyward, seeking a formation of clouds to animate the scene she wanted to capture. Her eyes, her lenses, ever sought to bring movement into her photos, to document the constant, often imperceptible changes in nature. At times Mami would ask us to stand near a tree or sit on a stump as a focal point in the expanse of nature, to highlight the contrast between far and near.

Portrait of Julie Meiners-Bölken. Photo by Hans Saebens, ca. 1940.

In my mind's eye I see other close-ups of my mother: the competent woman, a photojournalist, at ease with business associates as she is with Worpswede's artists, her friends and neighbors. Mami is attractive and stylish, she is kind, she is witty, she likes to laugh, but she is always controlled. Mami appears sure of herself, perhaps even a little arrogant as she retains a barely noticeable distance from others. I see her walking with a relaxed yet determined step in the village or along the moor paths to visit the peat farmers whose work and environment are among her favorite photographic subjects. And yes, I see Mami, our mother, at home with us at mealtimes and during evenings, talking and listening. She is not cooking or baking, she's not doing the laundry or cleaning the house, she's not sewing, but she is at the center of our home. She is the person who makes us a family and sets the tone of kindness and thoughtfulness, who creates a safe environment for us, something we undoubtedly took for granted. Of course, I'm aware that my recollections may be based on a subconscious wish for constancy, a state of being that doesn't want acknowledge change — be it the wish of the child or adult.

However, preceding the move to Worpswede in early summer of 1931, our family had come face-to-face with significant changes in our lives, the major change being my parents' divorce. Since I was only three years old at the time of their separation my recollections of home and family events while the whole family lived in the town of Erfurt are faint. I also don't recall a difficult transi-

A brief rest during a morning "photography" walk with our mother: Christa, Charly and Angela. Photo by JMB, Worpswede, ca. 1936.

tion from a life with both parents to living without our father. I
do know that Papi's work required frequent traveling and thus
he was seldom part of our daily routine. Does this explain why
I, along with my sisters, adjusted easily to his complete absence
and our new living and family condition? What I do remember
is a close family consisting of our mother, two older sisters and
our housekeeper Hille, a young woman who had been part of our
family since before my birth.

What are among my first memories of our surroundings in
Worpswede? I can still visualize the gabled house, surrounded
by many trees, which my mother had rented in the *Donhorst*
section, less than a mile from the center of the village. This rural
area, sparsely populated by small farms, led to a large peat bog, a
moor, where peat farmers lived and worked in a silent, dark brown
landscape, interspersed with rows of white birches. From spring
throughout the summer the families of peat farmers -- husband,
wife and children -- worked to cut and dry peat. It was hard work.
By the end of the summer the dried peat was moved by wheelbar-
row to nearby narrow canals intersecting the moor. There the peat
was loaded onto roughhewn dark brown boats and poled down the
canal to the river Hamme, from where they sailed under brown
sails to nearby towns and cities, eventually arriving in Bremen.

Other memories are of horses with their empty wagons rum-
bling on the unpaved roads past our house. During the hay harvest
the wagons would be filled with fragrant grass that had been cut and
slowly dried on the meadows surrounding the village. Family lore
has it that I loved visiting neighboring farms where I was treated to
home-baked bread and liverwurst and that my first language was
Plattdeutsch ('flat' German), a dialect spoken by the farmers in the
region. I have vivid memories of our friendly neighbors and the
delicious sandwiches, but I don't remember speaking *Plattdeutsch*

A row of loaded peat boats on the river Hamme on their way to Bremen.
Photo by JMB. ca. 1940

— I evidently lost the dialect as soon as I entered first grade. *Auf der Donhorst* was a safe neighborhood for children because the occasional horse and wagon and bicycle riders moved at a slow pace. Therefore, my sisters and I were allowed to explore and visit our neighborhood — all of it was home. My grandmother, *Grossmama Bölken,* who visited us off and on, loved to exclaim "how idyllic," and I am sure she described our living and environment well.

Around the time I started school we moved into a house closer to the center of town—a new environment for us. I remember the house, the yard, the vegetable garden and the meadows that stretched beyond the back of our house. There were new neighbors, a mailman who was also our neighbor, and some children my age with whom I played. Around that time, Lotte joined our family after Hille married, but she could never replace Hille. Our eccentric grandmother and an uncle visited us off and on. I remember playing with my sisters, although, as the youngest I just tagged along more than being a participant. I remember learning to read and write, learning to ride a bicycle, enjoying playing in the soft black mud of the unpaved road in front of our house for which I was severely scolded by Lotte. I remember a fall when my sisters and I had whooping cough and how annoyed Lotte was by our constant coughing. I remember flags flying along the few streets in the village—at first just the striped flag of red, white and black and then the swastika flag that, with its large area of blood red, seemed threatening. I remember accompanying my mother to the voting booth in the public school—she was quiet and looked very serious. Among the varied memories is the quiet and loving presence of my mother, a presence even when she had to be at work or out-of-town on photographic assignments. I felt safe.

However, despite this sense of wellbeing and safety, I recollect that our early years in Worpswede were shadowed by financial difficulties. An example of this awareness is my clear memory of pan-fried potatoes, a staple in our home. The potatoes were fried in grease that tasted simply horrible. Its aftertaste stayed with us for hours. I think it was my sisters who told me that the grease was inexpensive and that I should not complain. How did they know that? Of course, they were a few years older than I and probably overheard conversations about household expenses between Mami and Hille. I am certain that my mother's original income as a photographer's assistant was small. Much later I learned that our father wasn't able to make any financial contributions to our household during those years. I assume that my mother's father, our *Großpapa Bölken*, helped out with expenses, but with her strong sense of independence my mother probably tried to handle things on her own as much as possible. Certainly, in her calm and friendly way she surrounded my sisters and me with a sense of assurance that all was well. For that matter, I don't think that we were of an age to take on the worries of adults, but lived within the charmed circle of the confidence of children.

This vision didn't change much over my earliest years. The fleeting memories I have retained from our life before we moved to Worpswede, a time when we lived with both parents and Mami was with us full time, seem to have merged with the new day-to-day experiences. Then, when my mother started to work full-time and was gone most of the day my sisters and I were in the caring hands of our housekeeper Hille, a loved and trusted friend. For years, after she married and raised her own family and our family dispersed to the United States and Chile, we continued to stay in touch with Hille by letter and a visit whenever we returned to Worpswede.

After having lived in Chile for over twenty years Mami returned to Worpswede in 1971 and re-established the close connection with

Our beloved friend and housekeeper Hille bundling rye during the harvest.
Photo by JMB. ca. 1936

Hille who still lived in the village. As young women, my mother as "the lady of the house," and Hille, hired to help with the household tasks and young children, had become friends. They shared being separated from their earlier homes, from their parents and siblings and the familiar area of northern Germany. The young women continued to depend on each other after the move to Worpswede in 1931. This bond was never broken. Germany, as I recall, was a class-conscious society with traditional demarcations between employer and employee. However, this separation apparently did not exist for my mother. I know that Mami grew up with many servants, but I believe that her parents' relationship with their domestic help was one of respect and kindness. Mami in turn taught us by example to extend friendship to neighbors and newcomers and I am certain we never considered it unusual. However, when as a teenager I began to be cognizant of the differences in power relationships, I fully appreciated my mother's honest and open connection with people from all different spheres of society and environments. Although my mother retained a certain distance from others, she was never condescending.

The last time I saw Hille was in November of 1988 on the occasion of my mother's 85th birthday celebration in Worpswede. Hille, then in her late seventies, a bit bent and slow on foot, yet with her ever kind and expressive eyes, climbed the stairs to Mami's apartment to congratulate her with a large bouquet of fall flowers from her bountiful garden. I remember one last embrace,

Who was Julie Meiners-Bölken, this calm person, this individual who, untrained and with few funds, set out to create a life for herself and her children in Worpswede? How did she prepare

herself for the demanding responsibilities as mother of three young daughters, as photographer, friend and mentor? What were her skills? What was in her background that gave her the strength and self-assurance to move forward?

Mami, born in 1903, grew up in the Hanseatic City of Bremen, a city fourteen miles north-northeast from Worpswede. Her father was an importer and he afforded his wife, my mother and her two brothers a comfortable life. I have an old photo album that shows the Bölken family at rest and at play in the Birkenhof, their large home, surrounded by park-like gardens. A year after the end of World War I, in 1919, when my mother was sixteen years old, her parents separated. The children remained with their father in Bremen. Her mother, deeply impacted by the brutality and horror of World War I, moved away from Bremen, lived in a simple apartment in Darmstadt and completely separated herself from her past, although she continued the communicate with her children by writing frequent letters.

Even though Mami seldom referred to her youth, it is clear that her mother's decision to leave the family was a life-changing event for each member of her family. Was it this experience that generated within my mother the determination to become self-reliant and independent? Did her father's keen interest in photography lead her to her first job as a photographer's assistant? Aside from the barest outlines of changes in Mami's family, my sisters and I never learned much about her youth, about her discovery of Worpswede, about the courtship and marriage of our parents, and what led Mami to her life's decisions. I believe that the culture of the time neither suggested nor encouraged the sharing of personal information, even within a close family circle.

As I am trying to retrieve information about Mami's youth, about her dreams and her reality, I realize that I am relying on bits and pieces of overheard conversations, on my own observations and a good measure of imagination. Even in later years, when my sisters and I were adults, our mother seldom spoke of her youth in personal terms. She did not share much about her life and hopes as a young woman nor about what precipitated the choices she made as an adult. She was a private person. Yet I continue to chide myself for not having been a more persistent questioner during the later years of her life. Wasn't I interested in her history or did my own developing life consume me to the extent that I forgot to ask more questions? A few years before Mami's death in 1991 I encouraged her to tape some of her memories, but she was not interested. Indeed, she remained a private person.

And then a surprise! Just a few days ago I rediscovered and finally took time to carefully look at and peruse a small hand-bound journal of photographs and writing that had belonged to my mother. This small piece of her past, recently found among her remaining possessions in her apartment in Temuco, Chile, was given to me by my sister Charly. The first page of the booklet is inscribed with the words: *Erinnerungen* (Memories)—*Worpswede 1918-1920,* and at the bottom of the page, the name *Julie Bölken— Bremen.* The album and its inscription tell me that Mami had visited Worpswede when she was only fifteen years old. How had she discovered Worpswede? Was it her mother who had originally been drawn to Worpswede and its artists and later introduced her children to the art colony? How did they get there? Most likely they traveled by train. Perhaps they sometimes went by bicycle? How was the teenager Julie introduced to the young people in Worpswede, some of them budding artists, who became her life-long friends? No, neither my sisters nor I will ever know anything about Mami's first acquaintance and deepening friendships with the young artists of Worpswede, for she and her friends are long gone. However, I can let my imagination roam and project that her first visits, along with the developing friendships, opened up a whole new world for her—a place where art and nature were central to life.

A further assumption: the careful grouping of her young friends, women and men, their names carefully recorded under each photo in the newly-found album, may be proof of my mother's interest in photography. Along with the photos a few pages of writing confirm her early, strong connection to the art colony. The album tells me that the young Julie Bölken came to love Worpswede, its focus on the arts and an attendant aura of idealism among the young people she met. I'm envisioning that the village must have become her refuge during the turbulent years when her mother withdrew from husband and children, first in spirit and then by physically moving away. This leads me to reflect on my mother's choice of returning to the community after her marriage ended. I believe that Mami sought Worpswede out as her and our new home as the place that some years earlier had already been her shelter.

The booklet is a gold mine, not only because of the unexpected discovery of Mami's early acquaintance with Worpswede and the photographs of her friends, but also because of the few of pages of her writing, a selection of epigrams: *Wahrheiten in kurzen Worten* —Truths in Brief Words. I treasure her notations as a key to her thoughts and ideals when she first encountered and became acquainted with Worpswede and its artists.

Art mediates the inexpressible.
Art occupies itself with the dilemmas of life. The dilemmas grow the closer you get to your objective.
I don't care for the artist who is not in harmony with his work.

Criticism is easy; art is difficult.
In each artist lies the seed of boldness
without which a talent cannot be expressed.
A friend is like another self, an alter ego.
The knot of friendship, not tied to wisdom,
is easily undone by foolishness.
Be true to yourself.

Mami's handwriting, even at the young age of fifteen, is distinct and determined. I try to imagine the strong feelings of the young Julie as she expresses herself on paper–probably in solitude. I don't hear her pronounce her thoughts in public. Is that because I can only remember her as a quiet, private person? Perhaps she was more demonstrative when she was younger? There is so much about my mother I don't know.

A second section in the small book, covering the years 1931 to 1932, includes several more pages of photographs of many of the same friends from earlier years. It also contains a single larger picture of the photographer who became her mentor and intimate friend. In this section she neither adds commentary nor does she identify anyone by name. Silent pages. Mami knows the stories.

The journal draws me again and again. I want to study the photographs of the groupings of young people. No photograph of Julie Bölken, the photographer, is included. The photos are a record of a time long gone, holding fast to the moments when the happy group of friends assembled for the photographs—moments that I can revisit at any time. They help me to visualize my mother as a young girl—perhaps laughing and finding release from difficult times. In the faces of Mami's friends I recognize the faces of the parents of my eventual school friends, thus confirming my own early memories of living in Worpswede.

Although the journal contains many empty pages a number of the photographs help me to fill the large gaps of knowledge I have about my mother's youth. Among them are photos and a name, which to this day are still very familiar. It is the name of Bettina Vogeler, the daughter of Heinrich Vogeler, one of the founders of the art colony. Her face—among a group of friends -- and her name represent the strong connection between Mami's discovery of Worpswede in 1918 and our move to the village in 1931, for Bettina and her family, her husband Walter Müller and their two children, Bettina and Hans Georg, became and remained close friends of our family for years to come. By now most of the original Vogeler-Müller family and my mother are gone—only Hans Georg still lives and works in Worpswede and we continue to stay in touch. A bridge that has stayed intact for nearly one hundred years.

While I'm delighted to have discovered something about my mother's youth I continue to be aware of my dearth of knowledge. I have to admit myself that, except on rare occasions, she was not given to reminiscing and seldom spoke of events during World War I and the years that immediately followed. Her reluctance to re-visit the emotionally turbulent years after her mother left her husband and her three children was certainly understandable. However, in August 1939, just before the start of World War II, Mami spoke to my sisters and me about her mother's decision to become a vegetarian during World War I and the impact it had on her children, who, especially toward the end of the war, experienced hunger on a daily basis. Mami recalled finding her way into her home's storehouse of smoked meats and sausages—forbidden territory as far as her mother was concerned. On that day the child Julie made herself violently ill by eating a whole liver sausage. No, her mother did not punish her, for it was clear that the experience of being sick was enough punishment. However, she made sure that meat of any kind was removed from the home and storehouse as of that day. I remember that my sisters and I were struck by the harshness of our grandmother's action. How was it possible that her decision to be a vegetarian was forced on her hungry children? Mami told us, without rancor, that until the end of World War I the family's diet was the same as the diet of most people—cooked or raw turnips and bread into which ground tree bark had been baked. We were horrified. I believe that the imminent approach of World War II released some of Mami's childhood memories; perhaps she was trying to prepare us for the hungry days that lay ahead.

Other questions come to my mind: when and how did our parents meet? Assuredly it was in Bremen, for our father was also born and raised in Bremen. From a book of family records, given to me some years ago, I know that our parents were married in Bremen in January of 1924. By that time our father must have completed his law studies. He may have worked in Bremen for a while, but already later that year he worked in Eisenach (Thuringia) where Charly was born. In 1926 my parents returned to Bremen–Angela's birthplace. Another move took them to Waldenburg where I was born in 1928. The last family residence, prior to our move to Worpswede, was Erfurt. The dates of our parents' marriage and their children establish all that I know of that time and place. No narrative accompanies the record book— and I have to leave the unwritten chapters there.

Worpswede was not only new chapter—I think it was the beginning of a new book. From my perspective the word Worpswede expresses everything that influenced our mother's life and in turn my sisters' and mine. The physical landscape—the moor, the birches, the sky with its clouds—continue to be ever-present in my life. Mami must have shown us by her own conduct that nature was our home as much as the house and the community we lived in. Of course, my mind also recollects pictures of good friends and friendly neighbors, of comfortable living rooms, bedrooms and playrooms, stairwells, attics and basements, as well as kitchens. I also retain visions of many happy celebrations such as Christmas, birthdays, Easter and Mother's Days in Worpswede. Yet the outdoor spaces, among them gardens, paths and roads, as well as hills around and beyond the village, leading to school, to the river and the mysterious moor, to the garden where we pulled weeds and enjoyed summer meals, to the places where we met our friends, went walking, swimming, sledding and skiing, these outdoors spaces remain the sites to which the memories of my childhood, of Mami and my sisters, are most closely connected.

In each memory frame I am looking for the individual, for Julie Meiners-Bölken, who is our mother—definitely OURS—and I see the attractive, strong woman, the creative and respected photographer. Her ability to observe, assess and choose sights to evoke the story of nature and people was remarkable and led to a successful career. I choose to believe my mother was defined by the combination of a protected and love-filled childhood followed by the sudden demand to mature when only in her teens. Did this background lead to her development into an independent woman? I know that I was immensely proud of Mami and thankful that I had such an accomplished and handsome mother, a woman who did not waver in the face of difficult decisions. She was a woman of courage and grace. In particular, this became evident to me during the Hitler years and World War II.

I know that Mami was never a follower. Independent thinking and action guided her life—fear did not seem part of it. She did not follow the Nazi ideology and had the courage to raise us in the same vein. I am grateful to Mami that she had enough trust in us to let us know, more often through her own actions rather than by words, that hate, betrayal and brutality, the hallmark of Nazism, were not acceptable. I was only five years old when Hitler came to power, but I remember being able to recognize the unjust actions of the Nazi dictatorship only a few years later. My mother raised us to be independent and yet considerate of others—not to hate, but to be aware of injustice and cruelty.

Mami's vision of life, of her work and actions continue to influence my life. Her quiet determination, exemplified by her firm but light step, as she followed the demands of her work as a photojournalist and daily tasks have left their indelible mark on me. At times she displayed a certain severity, which expressed itself in an almost limitless self-control as she responded to personal disappointments. From brief comments I know of the sorrow caused by the divorce from our father. I'm also aware of the rift between her father and herself when she found herself in need of financial help during her brief marriage and our first years in Worpswede. There was the pain and sadness for all of us when, in 1942, the marriage to Mami's mentor and colleague in Worpswede was called off. Soon after this up she experienced the loss of her mother -- the mother who chose a life of self-expression, that at least outwardly, excluded the care of her children. There must have been other sorrows in her life. In each case Mami continued without any obvious display of grief—I do not retain a vision of a frayed, unhappy woman. Did she summon this self-control to protect us or had she been brought up not to show emotion in front of others? Mami always appeared the strong one, the person who managed to look serene, although serious, even when she must have been hurt. Somehow she gathered the needed strength to focus on the beauty of life and combined it with a balanced approach to surmount the difficulties and disappointments, which inevitably faced her. She was a remarkable woman who was able to remain true to her ethics and ideals and thus lead my sisters and me to survive the Third Reich and World War II.

The powerful memory of Mami's manner of raising us with few words resurfaces again and again. Although we must have been lively children, full of questions and demands, I don't recall that Mami was impatient, talkative or given to long explanations. Despite her silences she made us fully aware of the beauty of our natural environment and the remarkable people who shared our world. Her strength was observation and the ability to see and reach beyond the ordinary, a gift she generously offered to us.

EPILOGUE
Brunswick, Maine, September 22, 2009

Of course, there is much more to the story of my mother—too much to share at this time or ever. Along with personal success Mami faced challenges and health problems. Fear and uncertainty, although carefully managed, must also have been part of her daily life. However, the most difficult challenge she confronted at the end of the war was to live with and share the knowledge of Germany's responsibility for the horrors of the Holocaust and the shattering of millions of lives across the world with us. How did Mami help us to gather strength, restore hope and learn to trust people again during those first post-war days, weeks and months? Each hour of each day was a challenge—emotionally and physically. Throughout the days of shame and pain Mami guided us with structured and purposeful living—planting our garden, restoring an old farm-house and caring for one another with or without conversation. I remember few words, but by then I knew that words couldn't always tell the story.

As the chains of dictatorship and war were removed the communal life in Worpswede changed. Before long many of us set out on individual paths in our newfound freedom -- moving back into the cities where the fear of bombs was now removed. Others, I among them, moved even further away. At the end of June in 1947 I left home and family for the United States and my marriage to Pete, an American soldier I had met the year before. Two years later, in the summer of 1949, my mother and two sisters moved to Chile, to be near Mami's younger brother Marcus, who had moved the city of Santiago in 1928.

Leaving Worpswede, Mami's physical and spiritual home for many years, was very difficult for her. Despite close family members, new friends and a lively interest in her new environment, the culture and language of Chile never became home to her. In 1971 Mami returned to Worpswede and discovered that despite having been away for twenty-two years the community was still home. The strong connection to her long friends of long ago, to the natural environment and the spirit of the artist colony remained unbroken. I believe that her appreciation for it had even deepened during the years of absence. To know that Mami was "at home" again was a relief and joy for the whole family. Worpswede and the memories of my youth, re-anchored by our mother's presence in the village, were strengthened for me as well.

In the mid-1980s Mami was diagnosed with breast cancer. She survived an operation and further treatment and decided to remain in Worpswede, surrounded by a few relatives, many friends and occasional overseas visits from my sisters and me. However, when her cancer returned a few years later the decision was made that she return to Chile where she would be able to live with my sisters Charly and Angela and get the medical care she needed. Could she have come to the United States and live with me? Yes and no—the "yes" refers to being welcome to live with me and my family in Brunswick; the "no" refers to the reality of the expense of health care in this country, which we could not have covered. Brutal!

I was able to visit Mami in Temuco, Chile in early November of 1991. Although we spent many hours together we carefully avoided the topic of the visible ravage and certain outcome due to her cancer. We played a game of make-believe based on the decision by the immediate family, perhaps owing to a certain culture, Chilean or family-devised, that no one would refer to the presence of the invasive cancer. I remember Mami's words: "I don't know what is wrong with me." Yet I was certain that she knew very well. I felt so dishonest when I kept silent and did not answer her question. I was dishonest. Yet I clung to the belief that I had to abide by the decision of the rest of the family members who would be at her side each day while I would be far away in my home in Brunswick. The painful memory of this lack of truthfulness has stayed with me.

Mami and I gently hugged each other before I returned home to Brunswick in mid-November—close to a month before she died. I knew that my loving sisters Charly and Angela, as well as Mami's nieces, nephews and grandchildren were there to care for her. Yet knowing that I could not accompany her until the end of her life was difficult. I am left with sadness and regret not only about our parting, but also with the knowledge that Mami could not end her life in her beloved Worpswede and rest among her many friends in Worpswede's *Friedhof* (yard of peace)—the familiar cemetery of flower gardens, shrubs and trees, so carefully tended by each generation since 1759.

Rest in Peace!

Desolate barracks and inner courtyard in Die kleine Festung (The Little Fortress), part of the concentration camp in Theresieustadt, Czech Republic. Photo by C. Meiners-DeTroy. 2003.

DESTINATION
THERESIENSTADT

Monday morning, September 29, 2003, at 8:30—I'm sitting in the train from Gemünden to Nürnberg, the first leg of my journey to Theresienstadt, a town known by its Czech name of Terezin since the re-establishment of the independent country of Czechoslovakia at the end of World War II. Czechoslovakia gave way to two independent countries—the Czech Republic and Slovakia—in a political split in 1993. In my diary entries I use the names Theresienstadt and Terezin interchangeably: the former refers to the town's history as a brutal concentration camp; the latter refers to the current reality of a town living apart from its devastating history.

I am apprehensive as I begin my journey to the Czech Republic. I feel a sense of dread about my encounter with the Holocaust on the grounds of the infamous ghetto town and concentration camp Theresienstadt—the small town that housed thousands upon thousands of political prisoners during the years of the Third Reich. Until now I have visited Germany's concentration camps in books and articles, numbing and devastating experiences, from the safety of my home. However, today I am not reading about the horror and brutality. Today I am traveling toward Terezin to visit the site of the camp where my former neighbor, Frau Abraham, was murdered—and I am fearful of facing the pain and shame. Tomorrow, when I get off the bus and walk through the ghetto town, when I take my first step through the gate which leads into the interior of "*Die kleine Festung*" (The Little Fortress), I will be forced to go beyond my fragmented childhood memories of Frau Abraham, a small woman always dressed in dark clothes, and my farewell visit with her in November of 1939. Sixty-four years later I still remember the questions of the naïve eleven-year old girl who wondered why no one lifted a finger to prevent her deportation and why the people of Germany, willingly and/or by feigning ignorance, surrendered their Jewish neighbors to an uncertain fate. Today I am older than Frau Abraham was at the time of her disappearance, yet despite my living and learning during those years I am still asking the same questions. Can I expect to gain insight, perhaps a sense of understanding of past history when I step into the locus of the Holocaust in Theresienstadt?

Why am I traveling to Terezin? Three years ago, when I was engaged in the research on the life and disappearance of Frau Abraham and discovered that she and her two sisters-in-law had perished in Theresienstadt, I told myself that I must visit the concentration camp sometime in the future. I felt compelled to come face to face with Frau Abraham and her death; I wanted to apologize to her and her remaining family, to ask their forgiveness for abandoning her. As my research into the Holocaust and the life of Frau Abraham expanded she became more than my lost neighbor; she became a symbol for the millions of innocent men, women, and children who were abducted, terrorized, and murdered during the Holocaust. I realized then that my visit to the concentration camp was an essential part of acknowledging my personal responsibility, as a human being and a person born in Germany, for the crimes against humanity.

How does one prepare one's mind and soul for an encounter with a concentration camp? Just a few minutes ago, when I was boarding the train in Gemünden, the emotional strain of what lies ahead almost overwhelmed me. Not only do I question my earlier decision to visit Theresienstadt, I also question whether I have a right to step back in time and walk within the space where Frau Abraham lived out her life. Will I dare to visualize the daily degradations and humiliations imposed on her and other prisoners by people who could have been my neighbors? Can I stand face to face with the corporeality of the Holocaust or will I want to turn my eyes away? Who has given me permission to intrude into this private space made sacred by the suffering of innocent people? The questions keep coming as my thoughts race ahead to Theresienstadt and, just as quickly, return to Worpswede and my farewell visit with Frau Abraham. Did we say *Auf Wiedersehen* on that gloomy Sunday afternoon in November and did we believe that we would see each other again? I am certain that neither Frau Abraham nor I could have imagined what was facing her and that she would never return home. Suddenly I realize that the journey I've embarked on today will be my second good-bye visit to her; not to say *Auf Wiedersehen,* for it is too late for that but to acknowledge her life and suffering, and to let her family know that she is not forgotten.

Some of the practical aspects of my trip to the Czech Republic are also intimidating. For one, I don't know the Czech language. I will not be able to start a conversation with someone; I will not be able to establish human contact and develop a connection across borders and cultures. How will I, a stranger and tourist, find my way around Prague and Terezin? Should I speak English or German when I ask for directions? Last night, before setting out on this trip, my son Daniel and I discussed the language question and we agreed that it would be better to use English. No, I won't hide my German origins behind the English language, but at the same time I don't want to be the cause of reawakening painful memories of German occupation. In my mind I've repeatedly gone over what it will be like to visit a country that suffered for years under German oppression. Will anyone want to turn me away? What will it feel like to be seen as a tourist, whether German or American—a stranger who comes to stare at something unfamiliar or too familiar, someone who may take some pictures, perhaps buy a few souvenirs and then leave? However, even though I fall into the category of tourist and stranger, someone who will spend only a few hours in an unfamiliar town, I don't come to stare. I've come to pay my respects to Frau Abraham. I've come to pray for forgiveness and peace.

As I begin this journey I feel alone, almost abandoned, even though I reassure myself that God is with me, and I know that I'm surrounded by the thoughts of family and friends. Facing the horror and shame of the concentration camp alone is not easy. However, from the day I decided to visit Theresienstadt it was clear to me that I wanted to go there by myself. I knew that I needed to experience the camp in silence, without any commentary, without any intercession by a family member or friend. I need to meet Frau Abraham alone.

Since yesterday morning, when Daniel, his family, and I attended a church service in Würzburg, I have felt like crying—for Frau Abraham and for everyone who died or lost a loved one in the Holocaust; for everyone who has tried to silence the memory of the Holocaust; for those who cannot acknowledge their complicity yet are forever burdened by a memory that cannot be erased. While surrounded by the music and words of the religious service celebrating Yom Kippur, the Day of Atonement, the reality of my undertaking sank in deeply. Now, as I am sitting in the train, I swallow hard and try to gain control over my emotions. I focus on God and look for assurance that the journey to Theresienstadt is the one I must take—I've not felt this fearful for many years.

The last time I traveled with apprehension and fear was in September of 1946, on the day when I traveled from northern to southern Germany to visit my American fiancé Pete, who was stationed in Oberammergau. During that trip I was flung into the chaotic post-World War II world when overcrowded trains frequently broke down or ran out of coal; when people, made ruthless by hunger, fear, and abandonment, preyed on each other for space, food and any sign of material possessions. On that day I feared for my life as strangers coldly stared at me while I tried to sit unobtrusively in the dirty, overcrowded waiting room of Hannover, hoping that another train would be put into operation before too many hours passed. Sullen, hopeless and homeless young and old men, disgorged from the recent war, wearing odd combinations of torn uniforms and civilian clothes, brazenly looked at my wristwatch and knapsack, as if ready to kill me for my few possessions. Today is a different day and I am filled with a different kind of fear, for I do not fear for my life and I do not fear other people. Today my deeply felt angst focuses on my inner life and what lies ahead of me. I pray for strength and endurance.

I want to be strong as I face Theresienstadt and Frau Abraham, but what does it mean to be strong? Does it require an unreadable face and a tensed heart? Can I hide my emotions? No, I am not a Stoic. I don't want to hide my feelings—I can't hide them. I know that it's all right to cry, to mourn, to feel ashamed and helpless at the memory of sanctioned brutishness and murder. I need to feel free to acknowledge the life and death of Frau Abraham with tears. I wish I would have known how to put a safe space around her in the fall of 1939, a space in which she could have been protected, surrounded by respect and love—I wish I could put my arms around her now.

My thoughts veer off again as I ask myself for the thousandth time: "What drove people to become 'willing executioners' in service to Hitler and National Socialism?" In my search for answers, I have formulated dozens of responses and explanations based on history and psychology, but can any of them explain the why of the Holocaust? Are explanations nothing more than excuses? Enough of all of this—Frau Abraham was murdered, along with millions of other people. This fact cannot be sanitized by a carefully constructed academic theory. Kyrie eleison! God have mercy upon us!

10:28 A.M.—The first leg of my journey, from Gemünden through Würzburg to Nürnberg, has been completed. I've boarded another train, the train that will take me directly to Prague where I will stay overnight before continuing to my final destination—Terezin/Theresienstadt. The loudspeakers on the platform announce that we will be leaving shortly. I'm sitting in an old fashioned, stuffy compartment meant for eight people. For the moment I'm alone, but before long two women enter; both are Czech. We make room for one another; we nod at each other with smiles. The train starts to move. My journey continues.

One cannot pass through Nürnberg (Nuremberg), once the home of the well-known 15th-16th century artist Albrecht Dürer, without reflecting on the city's more recent history. Since the early 1930s Nürnberg was most closely associated with huge, flag-bedecked Nazi Party rallies, the "*Reichsparteitage*" that were attended by Hitler and his council of henchmen, as well as by thousands of screaming and cheering Germans. Appropriately, Nürnberg was chosen as the site of the post-World War II War Crimes Trials. The trials began on November 20, 1945, and were completed in the fall of 1946. Recently, as I re-read the 1946 decisions of the International Court, I discovered that it not only dealt with passing judgment on and sentencing German war criminals, but extended its deliberations to establish once and for all that "to plan or instigate an aggressive war is a crime under the principles of international law." The international tribunal further decreed, in response to the contention raised by most of the Nazi defendants that they could not be held legally responsible for their acts because they had followed the orders of their superiors, that "having acted on the authority of a superior, does not exempt a person from a moral responsibility for his act."

11:30 A.M.—The train is moving through small and medium-sized towns, past fields, forests, and hilly regions. In quick succession we pass through many short tunnels that briefly envelop us in complete darkness. Eventually the landscape changes and opens up into wide, level fields, many of them recently plowed. Europe has just gone through an unusually dry and hot summer and one can see the results as the train races past a drab and brownish landscape with only an occasional relief of the dark green of spruce forests. The settlements change as we travel east, moving from towns into more rural areas with occasional mid-sized farms. Shortly before our train crosses into the Czech Republic I notice two towers that unmistakably indicate the presence of nuclear power plants. The plant is located in Arzberg (Oberfranken), a mid-sized industrial town. The sight of the towers gives me a start, for not only do they trigger recollections of nuclear disasters in the U.S. and the former Soviet Union, but are frightening reminders of war and death. They also remind me of the mid-fifties' slogan "Atoms for Peace," and the years when the development for peaceful uses of atomic power received much attention. It was a time when Oak Ridge and other atomic research centers appeared to focus on the constructive uses of the new knowledge in order to support and increase post-World

War II industrial growth. With this development came the hope that the shift to "Atoms for Peace" signaled a national commitment to harness the power of the atom for peace—a response to international calls of "No more Hiroshimas! No more Nagasakis!"

12:10 P.M.—German border police enter each compartment and request passports from the travelers. The police carefully scrutinize the documents and repeatedly glance from the passport photo to the passport owner, as if they didn't trust their eyes—or didn't they trust us? With a polite "*Danke schön*" the border patrol leaves. Fifteen minutes later—we are now in the Czech Republic, in the town of Cheb—the Czech border police arrive and repeat the performance of their German counterparts. I can't understand their parting words, but, no doubt, they also said "thank you."

Although the countryside has not changed since crossing into the Czech Republic, there is a visible difference in the villages and towns I observe through the window. The towns we pass through appear to be dominated by rows of concrete apartment buildings—they have the appearance of government housing, hastily and cheaply built during the post-World War II housing crisis. The villages and isolated farmhouses amid the expanse of gray-brown, sun burnt fields, have the look of neglect and hopelessness.

12:50 P.M.—An indistinct voice informs us over a crackling loudspeaker—first in Czech, then in German and English—that all passengers have to disembark at the next stop, the town of Marianski Lazne (Marienbad). Due to repair work on a long section of the track ahead we are to be transported by bus to the town of Kozolupy where another train will be waiting to take us to Prague. Silently and orderly all of us get off the train and board the buses—it seems to me as if we could still be living under a dictatorship. I manage to get a window seat on the bus and strain to see as much as possible of the town and its forested hills as we

drive through winding streets. I remember hearing about Marienbad, the well-known spa, when I was a little girl. From the very
first time I heard the name "Marienbad" I envisioned a romantic
town, where kings, queens, and noblemen gathered to be pam-
pered, surrounded by elegance and beauty. Indeed, research tells
me that the spa, developed in the late eighteenth century, was made
famous by its opulent hotels and prominent patrons: European
royalty and internationally known composers and writers, among
them Chopin, Bruckner, Goethe, Kafka, Nietzsche, and even Mark
Twain. Today, more than fifty years since the end of World War II,
I observe that the spa, reopened in the late nineteen-forties, shows
the same post-war look of neglect and disrepair that is in evidence
along our travel route.

2:00 P.M.—The buses arrive in Kozolupy and we immediately
board the train to Prague. I have new travel companions—a silent
young man, three Czech women, and an American couple. We
help each other stow the heavy luggage on the racks above the seats.
Since most of us are older—the young man left the compartment
in a hurry when he saw the elders entering—lifting the bags is a
struggle. Many smiles and words of thanks in Czech, English and
German show that we appreciate each other's help—expressions of
kindness from one human being to another. If life were only that
simple! After we've settled down, the American couple and I get into
a conversation—both are retired teachers from Lewisburg, PA. Their
interests and work have taken them to various places around the
world; among them a year on the African continent as Peace Corps
volunteers. During the past three days they have visited Nürnberg
and now look forward to a four-day stay in the Czech Republic,
including a day-visit to Theresienstadt. Our conversation ranges
from reflections on Africa, the Nuremberg Trials, the Holocaust,
and Iraq. How can our lives hold and absorb that many experiences?

The countryside flies by—a parched landscape, brown and desolate. I realize that I've seen little if any human activity on the fields and roads, not even in Marienbad, since we've crossed into the Czech Republic. We're traversing an empty, silent land. Traveling by train for hours is a stark reminder of trains filled beyond capacity with deportees on their way to concentration camps in the Czech Republic and Poland during the 1940s. Although I've read many books and seen several films describing those endless and brutal journeys I will never know the dread and the pain of people who, thronged into cattle cars without food and drink or any facilities, were taken toward unknown destinations. Until early this morning I've unthinkingly identified train travel as a pleasant experience. Today this association vanishes in the face of the obvious connection between freely chosen train travel and the forced deportation of millions of people to death camps.

4:05 P.M.—Our train enters the busy Central Woodrow Wilson railroad station in Prague. Mechanically I disembark and join the crowd of passengers, all of us walking silently in an underground tunnel that leads into the station's central hall. I'm apprehensive as I try to find my way around the station, looking first for a currency exchange office and then for a taxi stand. Actually, I find both without difficulty. Outside the station I'm greeted by a group of taxi drivers, standing and talking alongside their cabs. When I give the address of the small hotel where I will spend the night the drivers appear to draw lots among themselves to decide who will take me there. Is the fact that my destination is either too short a ride to make it worthwhile or outside the city where it will be difficult to find a fare back to the station the reason for their haggling? Or am I an unwanted intruder—the identity I fear. Eventually the drivers make a decision and I'm driven to Prokopka Pension, not far from the center of the city. When I introduce myself to the receptionist at the front desk I face another moment of uncertainty, for she informs me that she does not have a reservation for me. Is this possible? Another refusal? Then, after searching through her computer, the receptionist tells me that the pension has an empty guest room after all.

By the time I enter my room, a small room, bare but clean, it is already after 5 p.m. I crane my neck as I look out of the window of my second-floor room, hoping to see something of the beautiful city of Prague. However, my window faces a narrow, empty court-yard with adjoining windowless buildings of indiscriminate colors and peeling stucco. Everything looks barren and neglected. After a short rest I step out into Prokopka Street—a busy commercial street of office buildings, shops and restaurants. Although it is now too late to venture into the city and visit historic sites I feel compelled to see something of Prague. Can I expect to get a sense of life of the city by walking down a few streets and peering at a few build-ings? I realize, just as I felt driven to study the countryside from the train window, I want to absorb some particulars about Prague and the Czech Republic, something that I can respond to, something to which I can connect. However, there is no connection, neither in terms of recognizing a familiar historical sight nor in terms of being able to exchange a greeting. I am truly an outsider.

Tuesday, September 30—7:00 A.M.—I am directed to the "breakfast room" in the basement of the pension, where, sitting down to a typical European breakfast of hard rolls, cold cuts and cheese, I meet other hotel guests, among them visitors from France, Norway, and the United States. Our common language is English; our common identity is that of the stranger. Although we sit at separate tables and don't exchange names, each of us seems eager to engage in conversation. A Norwegian teacher, accompanying a group of music students on their visit of Prague, tells me that they plan to travel to Theresienstadt on the following day. An American couple visiting their daughter in Prague will also make the trip later on this week. Is a visit to the concentration camp the focus of most foreign visitors to Prague?

8:30 A.M.—With my bag in hand I step outside and look at the gray fall sky—it's a gloomy day. A taxi arrives and takes me to the large Florenc Bus Depot. Using the fewest words: "*Praha-Terezin*" (Prague-Terezin) and "*Terezin-Praha*," I purchase a roundtrip ticket. Then, by pointing to entries on the bus schedule, the official at the ticket counter informs me from which platform and at which time the bus for Terezin will leave. I have more than thirty minutes to wait and look around the bus depot. There are at least thirty-five platforms—lined up in rows with three separate boarding sections. According to the signs the destinations range from local to international, especially to cities and countries to the east and south of the Czech Republic. One by one people queue up at #17 platform, the departure area for the bus to Terezin. In silence I observe and wait.

9:30 A.M.—The bus to Terezin pulls in and I join the crowd of locals and a group of French high school students and their teachers in boarding the bus. The vehicle is crowded, but I find an empty seat beside a young woman. The bus takes us through a series of small towns, open fields and hills; in the distance we see a mountain range—perhaps it is the Erzgebirge—the Ore Mountains—that I remember from my geography classes of long ago? Despite the presence of so many people on the bus there is little talking; only the bus driver's radio with its music, intermittent news reports, and advertisements breaks the silence. Occasionally the bus stops and discharges one or two passengers. We travel north for more than an hour. Suddenly, on my right, I see a large open field of gravestones with flowers placed between them. The bus comes to a halt as the French group gets off. I realize that this must be the Die kleine Festung, part of Theresienstadt's concentration camp, but I'm too stunned by the sight of the vast cemetery to get off. Everything within me convulses into shame and fear. The bus moves on, drives through the town—I assume it has to be Terezin—without stopping. I don't have the words to indicate to the driver that this is where I want to get off. The bus finally comes to a halt at its end station a few miles beyond Terezin. It is obvious that the few remaining passengers and I have to get off. What shall I do now? How do I get to my hotel? I walk to a nearby supermarket in the hope that I will find someone to ask about a taxi. In the store everyone is very busy, intent on shopping, not looking up and I can't catch anyone's eye. However, when I go outside again I notice a couple of women putting bags of groceries into their car and inevitably our eyes meet. My question concerning a "Taxe" is understood and the women respond with hand directions to the nearest taxi stand. The ride to the Park Hotel in Terezin takes only a few minutes. I have arrived at my destination.

Just as at the Propopka Pension in Prague there is no confirmation of my reservation at the Park Hotel in Terezin. It seems bizarre that this is the second hotel that is about to turn me away. Where will I be able to find sleeping accommodations in this small town? However, again I am lucky—the hotel has an empty guest room. It is close to noon by the time I unpack and settle into my still simpler and sparer room than the one in Prague, but I'm relieved that I can stay here for the night.

1:30 P.M.—A short walk from the hotel stands the *Ghetta Muzeum*, which, along with a small movie theater and souvenir shop, exhibits recent works of art by adults who as children had escaped the certain fate of their parents by being sent to England with a *Kindertransport*. The works of art are collages of fragments of their childhood—a pair of baby shoes, parts of clothing and toys, pages of a book or a letter, photos of parents, and their emigration documents. Each of the collages is a painful illustration of their broken and disrupted lives. I walk around and look at the framed pictures, numbed by the messages they extend. Actually, the whole town numbs me. I envision prisoners everywhere and the vision is accentuated by the drabness of this small town, whose large, square buildings still retain the look of officialdom and prisons.

After my visit to the museum I walk in the direction of Die kleine Festung. My eyes try to draw in every detail of the town, especially its barrack-like buildings and the blocks of apartment houses in which thousands upon thousands of innocent people—women, men and children—were imprisoned during World War II. In 1946 the buildings and houses were restored to their original use as private apartments for the then returning Czech population of Terezin. As I reflect upon the enormity of the post-war change I ask myself how the current occupants deal with the memories of terror and pain that are forever bound to these buildings? Have the families been able to create comfortable homes in the buildings of Terezin that, for a few years, were transformed into overcrowded tenements for a starving and terrorized prison population? I continue on my way to Die kleine Festung through a small, barren park and across a bridge, under which a shallow river barely moves. Without ceasing I think of Frau Abraham and that these same sights must have greeted her upon her arrival in the summer of 1942. I see everything, yet in reality I see nothing—I'm only aware of the oppressive environment and its sorrowful message.

Almost too soon I arrive at the field of memorial stones. Standing in front of the memorial arena I now recognize that the flowers between each stone are actually rosebushes—the color of their blossoms is cardinal red. The roses are beautiful, but they cannot alter the impact of desolation and grief of the hundreds of memorial stones, some with names and dates, many only with numbers. At the front of the memorial garden, dominating the field of stones and roses, stands a tall, dark-stained wooden cross. A crown of thorns is placed at the intersection of the vertical and horizontal beams. Clearly, it is the Christian symbol of suffering. Toward the end of the memorial garden, close to the entrance of the concentration camp stands the Star of David—the Jewish symbol. I question the location and size—one in front, the other further back, one large and one significantly smaller—of the two religious symbols. I question whether the large cross is appropriate in this arena. Although both Jewish and Christian prisoners perished at the camp I assume that the inmates were predominantly Jewish. Unfortunately, I cannot find anyone with whom I can speak about the juxtaposed symbols.

After walking through the prison complex of deteriorating barracks for some hours I decide to take a break on a bench in front of an art museum that is surrounded by birches and horse chestnut trees. I've discovered many horse chestnut trees inside the grounds of Die kleine Festung and in the town of Terezin. Because of the dry summer most of their leaves have already fallen on the ground; others, still clinging to the branches, are brown and dried up and ready to fall. The trees have a ghostly appearance with their dark, mostly bare branches, as they stretch out over the silent concentration camp. Suddenly I remember the large horse chestnut tree at the edge of our front garden in Worpswede. At the end of each summer my sisters and I would gather the shiny chestnuts and play with them. Now, as I discover chestnuts on the ground, shiny, not yet dried up, I decide to pick a few of them up and save them—my memento of Theresienstadt.

In the silence surrounding me I reflect on what I have seen

and felt during the past few hours. The sadness of Die kleine Festung is overpowering. An unremitting grief pervades everything around me. I've walked around the grounds of the fortress, walked up and down the courtyards that separate the rows of barracks; I have faced the entrance to one courtyard that bears the arrogant and cynical Nazi slogan *"ARBEIT MACHT FREI"* (labor frees) and I am drained. Retracing the steps of thousands of inmates is an out-of-body experience—my feet are moving automatically, as though I have no control over them. My eyes see but don't want to transmit the messages to the brain. The mind, the heart, want to block out the images of Frau Abraham and others who lived and died within the ghetto town Theresienstadt and within the grounds of this old fortress. My mind wants to erase the images of hunger, disease, and death—the images are obscene.

I'm conscious of having intruded into a sacred and private space. I feel like an interloper, a peeping Tom, vicariously witnessing the degradation and death of Holocaust victims. Much as I believe that concentration camps and other places of terror of Hitler's regime must be accessible as a reminder of what happened when a nation went mad, I now wonder about the invasion of tourists who, most often in groups, are channeled by tour guides through the barracks and surroundings. How can the guides communicate that Theresienstadt is more than a museum, more than an exhibit of the chards of a violent time?

I am not sure that Frau Abraham died in Theresienstadt. Only the names of her two sisters-in-law are documented in the Memorial Book, which supposedly lists all—or most—of the names of the victims of this ghetto town. This has been on my mind for some time. Should the few remaining descendants of Frau Abraham or I begin a search that would document the path to her death? What would it take? What would be the result? Would additional or different knowledge change anything? Would the measure of our pain increase if we imagine that she had to go undergo further hardships?

Suddenly, as I sit here, concentrating on what I have seen and felt, I arrive at an unexpected moment of clarity: I know that I must let the search for Frau Abraham rest right here, in Theresienstadt. Not only because I feel inadequate to further research her fate—was she transported to another camp before the end of the war?—but because I can't change history, I cannot undo her death, I cannot undo anything. I say to myself again and again: *Sie soll jetzt ihre Ruhe haben, sie soll ihren Frieden haben* (she needs to be left alone, she needs to be at peace)—because it is about Frau Abraham and not about those of us who are looking for more information about her. It's time to think of and honor the good parts of her life—her married life in Worpswede, her family and a grandson who deeply loved her. I have an old photo of Frau Abraham, her daughter and her grandson, sitting in the shade of a large linden tree in front of her comfortable home Am Richtweg. Her grandson presented me with this photo during my visit with them in the fall of 2000. A shaft of sunlight brightens the black and white photo of the smiling women and the small boy; a bouquet of flowers sits on the table between Frau Abraham and her daughter. It is a family scene; a scene that speaks of tranquility and I want to believe that much of her life was peaceful and comfortable. I try to convince myself that she wants her life to be remembered in this way.

5:00 p.m.—After my return to the hotel I take time to go over my notes of the past few hours in an attempt to translate the randomness of my thoughts and experiences into some sort of an understandable sequence. Putting thoughts into words is helpful to sort out feelings, yet the question of the why and extent of the Holocaust continues to overshadow everything—even after fifty-eight years since the end of World War II.

I reflect on Worpswede and Germany as a whole in connection with the Holocaust. Will the shame go on forever? Will there ever be a time of reconciling and forgiving? Can one ever dare to say: "It's done. The time has come when we must be able to live without recrimination." I ask myself if the shame and accusations will be put to rest after the last of the generation of those who were children during the Hitler years have died? In today's society a murderer, even if given a life sentence, is sometimes released from prison before he/she dies. Upon release it is said that he or she has paid his/her debt to society. Can one apply the same judicial process when a whole nation took part in the destruction and murder of millions of people? My answer: NO. I don't think it is possible. The dimensions of the Holocaust crimes exceed any possible comparison. Who has the right to be cleared of shame and guilt when the memory of its victims remains fresh in the minds of survivors and their families? Will there ever be a process in the future that will total up the debits and credits of the perpetrators and then can declare: "No outstanding balance?"

Does the youngest generation of Germans feel a sense of responsibility for the Holocaust? Do they say—as millions of white U.S. citizens did when, at the onset of the Civil Rights Movement in the nineteen-sixties, the deliberate crimes of slavery and segregation were finally publicly discussed—"this was not our doing; we cannot be held accountable for the actions of our parents, grandparents, and preceding generations?" At first glance this reaction, whenever and wherever expressed, may seem natural. However, in most instances these responses leave out the crucial part of acknowledging that a crime took place. I know that thousands of German school children visit the sites of concentration camps each year—I saw many groups of students at Die kleine Festung today—to acknowledge and confront the stark reality of what happened during the years of the Third Reich. How can we keep the unequivocal message of "Never Again" alive in the minds of the young people without passing on the shame and guilt of their elders? Are the older generations willing and able to help their descendants understand the difference between acknowledgement and evasion, between responsibility and guilt, without blurring the lines with defensive explanations and excuses and plain denial?

Before supper I decide to take another walk around Terezin. When I step outside I hear music in the distance and decide to follow the sound. Within minutes I arrive at an open field, where a small local band, grouped near a large sandbox, plays popular and traditional music. Mothers and children and a few young men make up the audience. The adults listen in silence, but the children are running around in the sand, having fun. I see a girl, perhaps eight years old, gathering other children into a circle. Clasping hands they dance, they tumble into the soft sand, they laugh, and get up again—a symbol of life and hope in this otherwise silent and somber town.

Postscript

In early April of 2004, while re-editing my essay, I decided to get in touch with a research institute in Prague with the primary motive to confirm some of my notes on the town and current population of Terezin. My request for information included a question concerning the approximate date of Rosa Abraham's deportation to Theresienstadt. Below is the brief and chilling report from the Terezin Initiative Institute:

Rosa Abraham, born on May 5, 1872, was deported to Theresienstadt on July 24, 1942, on the transport VII/I originating from Hannover, with the transport number 809. On September 23, 1942, Rosa Abraham was transported from Theresienstadt on the transport Bq, transport number 572, to Treblinka, where she was murdered.

Author's note: Later research revealed that her birthday was December 10, 1872.

AFTERWORD

Frau Abraham's life story did not end in Treblinka. Over several years my first essay about her life in Worpswede and her deportation to Theresienstadt was shared with a number of my friends and other residents in Worpswede. In the fall of 2012 a newspaper article about Frau Abraham and her recently deceased grandson Fred Goldschmidt reached members of the Foundation Worpswede. It was at that time that the foundation began to deliberate on how to honor the memory of Frau Abraham. Their final decision, supported by the local Village Council, called for the re-naming of a small park, a triangular meadow in the center of the village close to the last Abraham home.

On September 21, 2013, the park was officially named Rosa-Abraham-Platz in the presence of Irene Goldschmidt, Rosa Abraham's great-granddaughter, a large crowd of former and current Worpswede residents, several community leaders, members of my family and me. In my brief remarks to the gathering I expressed my thanks that Rosa Abraham had at last been returned to the consciousness and presence within the community. The decades-long silence surrounding Rosa Abraham's fate had finally been broken. It was an overwhelming experience.

A simple monument in the park tells her story in few but memorable words:

> Rosa Abraham, born on December 10, 1872, was a citizen of Worpswede who lived for many decades at what is now called Udo-Peters-Weg.
>
> In 1942 she was deported by the National-Socialist State to the Concentration Camp Theresienstadt—because she was Jewish.
>
> A short time later she was murdered at Treblinka.
>
> Other members of the Abraham family also became victims of Nazi persecution.
>
> This Platz is dedicated to her—as well as to other Jewish families—as a reminder of the crimes of the National-Socialist rule.

Photo by Tesia DeTroy.

Lightning Source UK Ltd.
Milton Keynes UK
UKHW021526110821
388640UK00010B/2052